With my warm regards

Frederick Merk

D0983686

HARVARD HISTORICAL MONOGRAPHS
XXIII

Published under the Direction of the Department
of History from the Income of

The Robert Louis Stroock Fund

HARVARD HISTORICAL MONOGRAPHS

Albert Gallatin *and* *the* Oregon Problem

A Study in Anglo-American Diplomacy

FREDERICK MERK

Cambridge: 1950

HARVARD UNIVERSITY PRESS

To

L.B.M.

K.L.M.

F.B.M.

PREFACE

For more than thirty years the Oregon question was a generator of tension in Anglo-American relations. From the time of the taking of Astoria in the War of 1812 to the Oregon Treaty of 1846 it produced incidents and crises, one after another, mounting in intensity. The earliest incident was the flare-up in England over the "Ontario" affair of 1817, when a United States sloop-of-war departed from New York for the mouth of the Columbia, unannounced to the British, for the purpose of asserting American sovereignty at the British-held site of Astoria. The second disturbance came in the period 1824-1826, when George Canning, the British foreign minister, was roused to anger so high by developments in the United States described in this narrative that Albert Gallatin felt it necessary to warn his government to make preparations for a rupture. The third was the war crisis of 1845-46, stirred up by the movement into Oregon of American pioneers and by the resulting American politics of expansionism.

In each of these crises a peacemaker happily appeared on one side or the other of the ocean to reduce fever and restore health. In the "Ontario" affair it was Castlereagh; in the disturbance of the 1820's, it was Albert Gallatin; in the war crisis of 1845-46 it was Lord Aberdeen. In each case the peacemaker was able to direct existing forces of good will and intelligence in the two countries to the reduction of emotion and the prevention of a rupture.

In this essay I have sought to assess the forces which made for rupture and those which made for peace in the second of these periods of tension. I have described them as focussed on the negotiation of 1826-27. The negotiation itself, less well known than it deserves to be, I have dealt with as an illustration of peacemaking in the process. I have conceived of it as a case study, a chapter in the history of the greatest problem facing mankind, the maintenance of peace among nations.

The peacemaker in this negotiation was Albert Gallatin. He succeeded almost singlehanded in rescuing the negotiation from failure and making it the means of lowering tensions. He was largely responsible for the relative quiescence that marked the Oregon issue in the period from 1827 to the end of the 1830's. He was one of the few American diplomats of his day who was respected on both sides of the Atlantic. He was regarded in England in 1826 as the sage of American statesmen. His association with the Oregon problem was as prolonged as the problem itself. He had watched, as a member of Madison's government and as a friend of Astor, the evolution of the Astoria enterprise. He was one of the American commissioners negotiating the Ghent Treaty of 1815, which provided for the restoration of Astoria. He was the principal American plenipotentiary at the conference of 1818, which framed the joint occupation. His services did not end with the conclusion of the negotiation of 1826-27. In 1846, at the height of the Oregon crisis, he published a series of quieting letters on the issue in the *National Intelligencer,* in which he suggested the line of boundary that was ultimately adopted. The letters were a profound influence for peace on that occasion on both sides of the Atlantic.

In these letters he briefly described diplomatists in their ideal character. In so doing he painted his own portrait as it will appear to the reader of these pages: "But, though acting . . . as advocates, diplomatists are essentially ministers of peace whose constant and primary duty is mutually to devise conciliatory means for the adjustment of conflicting pretensions, for the continuance of friendly relations, for preventing war, or for the restoration of peace."

The area that was at stake in the Oregon controversy was an imperial one. It extended from the Rocky Mountains on the east to the Pacific Ocean on the west, and from latitude 42° to 54° 40′. It embraced approximately 450,000 square miles, more than the combined surface of France, Germany, and Czechoslovakia in

1939. The area was destined to have future strategic importance for the United States and Canada. It became an outlet for both of them to the Pacific.

Five unsuccessful negotiations to partition this country took place between the United States and England before the final negotiation in 1846. Three of the five were in an early group, 1818, 1823-24, and 1826-27; two were of date shortly before and during the crisis of 1845-46. In the early negotiations each government began by proposing a line of partition and refusing the offer of the other. This interchange was repeated with little variation as the second negotiation followed the first and the third the second. By the time of the third, the subject of this essay, less than the whole area was in actual controversy. The controversy had been narrowed by the offers to a core—the triangle that lies between the Columbia River at the south and the 49th parallel at the north. This triangle was of importance to each contestant for its water appendages, the Columbia River on the one side and the harbor waters of the straits on the other.

The proposal which the American government made in the first three negotiations, the line of the 49th parallel to the sea, offered a reasonable basis for a settlement. With a slight alteration to avoid severing Vancouver Island and the straits, it was the line ultimately adopted as the boundary. It divided the deep water harbors of the straits as equitably as could be. It projected to the Pacific the boundary established in 1818 east of the mountains. It accorded well with the established claims of the two contesting powers. South of the line the claims of the United States, reënforced by those acquired from Spain, were far better than those of Britain. North of the line those of Britain were far the stronger. The line was the boundary that the finger of nature and the finger of history pointed out for the partition of the Oregon area.

In 1826 it was rejected by Canning. It had been rejected by him earlier. It was rejected in the interests of the transitory needs of the Hudson's Bay Company and the ambitions which Can-

ning had for the British Empire. The rejection meant the
storing up of a war crisis for the future, a crisis which was one
of a series that Canning's temper and policy created in Anglo-
American relations. Happily when the crisis occurred Lord
Aberdeen, a statesman of very different temper from Canning,
occupied the foreign office. Canning had been, so his critics
charged, a statesman of "talents without character." Aberdeen
was, preëminently, a statesman of character, and by him the
stubborn issue was finally laid to rest.

I wish to make special reference to a work recently published,
which briefly traverses the ground I have here covered, Samuel
Flagg Bemis, *John Quincy Adams and the Foundations of
American Foreign Policy* (New York, 1949). It is not referred
to in the text of this essay or in two companion pieces—"The
Genesis of the Oregon Question," *Mississippi Valley Historical
Review,* XXXVI (1949-50), 583-612, and "The Ghost River
Caledonia in the Oregon Negotiation of 1818", *American Historical Review,* LV (1949-50), 530-551, since it appeared after they
were all in typescript and the articles in the hands of the pub-
lishers. It is a notable contribution to the literature of American
diplomatic history and of the Oregon question. Its treatment of
the Oregon negotiation of 1826-27 will be found to differ widely
from mine. The differences arise to some extent from the fact
that we interpret the negotiation through different personalities
and philosophies, the nationalist philosophy and tense personality
of John Quincy Adams on the one hand, and the internationalist
philosophy and urbane personality of Albert Gallatin on the
other. The interplay of these great Americans upon each other
was as important to the nation and to the world in the Oregon
negotiation as it had been earlier at the Ghent peace conference.
It was a fortunate country that had two such minds balancing
each other on its behalf.

I am under many obligations for help in the making of this
study. In England I am under obligations to the staff of the
Department of Manuscripts of the British Museum, and especially to H. R. Aldridge, its assistant keeper. I have received special

courtesies from the staff of the British Public Record Office in Chancery Lane. I am indebted to the late third Baron Revelstoke for permission to use the Baring papers, then housed in London, and to the sixth Earl of Harewood for information regarding the George Canning papers. In Canada I am under obligation to the staff of the Public Archives at Ottawa for many courtesies, and especially to Dr. Gustave Lanctot, its Director. In the United States I wish to express my obligation to the staff of the Division of Manuscripts and the Division of Maps of the Library of Congress; to the National Archives; the William L. Clements Library; the New York Historical Society; the Peabody Institute of the City of Baltimore; the Massachusetts Historical Society; and the Harvard University Library. I am indebted to Albert E. Gallatin of New York City for facilitating my entrance into the papers of his ancestor in the New York Historical Society. The John Quincy Adams papers are not yet generally open to historians, but Henry Adams kindly made on my behalf a search through them for materials on my subject.

My greatest obligation is to my wife, Lois Bannister Merk, who read the manuscript of this book many times with a scholar's care. On almost every page I owe her a debt for keen and constructive criticism and invaluable help in my literary revision.

Frederick Merk

Harvard University
December 1949

CONTENTS

CHAPTER I

INCEPTION OF THE
LONDON CONFERENCE OF 1826-27

In April 1826 George Canning produced a stir in the American government by sending a note to the American minister in London. The note was a proposal to reopen the inconclusively ended Oregon negotiation of 1823-24. Canning gave no hint of his reasons for sending the note. In the game of diplomacy he was not the player prematurely to show his hand. But he gave an impression of urgency in the note by declaring that two British plenipotentiaries were ready to begin conferences at once, that they were prepared either to renew an offer which had been made in 1824, or to bring forward another, or to discuss any new offer the American minister might wish to make.[1] When the head of a foreign office thus presses the government of another state to reopen a negotiation that has recently failed, especially if the issue does not require immediate action, he produces a hope that concessions of importance are on the way. Such a hope Canning produced in the American government.

The reasons for the note were two. One was a Hudson's Bay Company need, set forth in a letter which the Governor of the Company had written Canning the preceding December.[2] The other was annoyance felt by Canning over developments in the United States. If the American government had known of these backgrounds of the note it would have been less hopeful than it was of the outcome of a renewed negotiation.

The Hudson's Bay Company was a partner of the crown in the building of the empire in North America. It had become

---

[1] Canning to King, April 20, 1826, *American State Papers, Foreign Relations*, VI, 645-646.

[2] See below, pp. 4-5.

a partner in 1670 when it obtained a grant of land from the crown. The grant was a vast one, the whole drainage basin of Hudson Bay. It extended westward to the crest of the Rocky Mountains, embracing the greater part of what is now Canada. It included not merely rights of soil but exclusive rights of trade. The Company named the grant Rupert's Land, in honor of Prince Rupert, a member of its directorate and a cousin of the King.

But the title of the Company to Rupert's Land was challenged. It was challenged first by the French. This was one of the issues fought over in the century-long Anglo-French duel in North America. In 1763 the duel ended with the expulsion of France from the continent. A new duel, however, followed. The Company's exclusive rights of trade were challenged by independent traders, especially by those organized as the North West Company. For another half century the Company fought the North West Company in a war that was bitter, increasingly violent, and ruinous to both. In 1821, at the behest of the government, the two companies finally, through a merger, made peace. The Hudson's Bay Company was able in the merger to retain its charter, its organization, and its name.

As a consequence of the merger the Company entered the Oregon Country. It acquired there the interests and position of the North West Company. It obtained, also, by gift from the government, a monopoly of all British rights of trade west of the mountains. The monopoly was a reward for the merger and an instrument for defeating American traders who might, under the terms of the joint occupation of 1818, undertake a competition. The Company was thus, in 1821, the sole British occupant of the Oregon Country. It was almost the only occupant of any nationality, for Americans were not crossing the mountains at all in those years to trap or trade.

For three years the Company took little advantage of its privileged position in its new sphere. It was engrossed in the immense task of reorganizing and rehabilitating its demoralized trade east of the mountains. It had to entrust the country west of the mountains to the former employees of the North West Company. These men, suspicious of the new regime and leaderless, served without energy. They permitted, in the lower Columbia, a trade deterioration to continue that had already set in before the merger. They allowed the lower Columbia to register, on the books of the Company, a succession of annual net losses. They led the directorate of the Company to regard the lower valley as a forlorn hope. The Company considered abandoning the lower river as a western base of operations and withdrawing northward to the Fraser.[3]

In the autumn of 1824 George Simpson, the American field governor of the Company, appeared at Fort George. He had come over the mountains from Hudson Bay for the purpose of surveying the Columbia Department and determining its future. He was a young Scot of lowly origin but high ability, who had been sent to America after the merger. He had already established a reputation in the East for driving power and administrative genius. He came to the West, surmising that the deterioration of the lower Columbia was the result of inefficiency, listlessness, and waste. He found these suspicions verified and applied the correctives with accustomed energy. He completely overhauled the Columbia Department, replacing its old head by a new one whom he had brought with him. The new head was Dr. John McLoughlin, an administrator as gifted as the Governor himself, who was destined to become a power in the affairs of the West and to dominate the Oregon Country for the next twenty years.[4]

One of Simpson's labors in the winter of 1824-25 was the dismantling of historic Fort George on the site of Astoria. This was done at the recommendation of Canning. The fort stood on a bank of the Columbia which was sure to go, in a future partition of the Oregon Country, to the United States. In its stead Simpson erected a new fort north of the river, opposite the mouth of the Willamette. He named the new establishment "Fort Vancouver," in order to associate the Columbia River explorations of the

[3] *Fur Trade and Empire,* Frederick Merk, ed., xxi-xxxi.   [4] *Ibid.*

Vancouver expedition with England's claim to the soil north of the river.[5]

These arrangements completed, Simpson was on his way back over the mountains in the spring of 1825. In the autumn he was in London ready to report on his activities and to make his recommendations. His recommendations were two. North of the Columbia, a vigorous program of expansion with a view to a permanent occupation of the country; south of the Columbia, a swift trapping out of the furs.[6]

An expansion north of the Columbia would involve a considerable outlay of capital and labor. The risks of such an outlay in an area of undetermined sovereignty, where national ambitions clashed, the Company well knew. It desired from the government, before committing itself irrevocably to the new program, an assurance that it would have the future use of the central transportation system of the Oregon Country, the Columbia River. More specifically it wished assurance that in a future partition of the Oregon Country the government would see to it that the river remained adjacent to British territory. If a partition on that basis could be arranged, the Company preferred it to the uncertainties of the convention of joint occupation. That convention was a ten-year arrangement which would shortly expire.

As a result of Simpson's recommendations, on December 9, 1825, the London governor of the Company addressed a letter to Canning. He gave an account of what the Company had done and what it proposed to do in the Oregon Country. He wrote of the expansion the Company contemplated northward from the Columbia and behind the mouth of the Fraser. He declared that for this expansion the Columbia would be necessary. The river was the highway by which the country behind the mouth of the Fraser and that on the Columbia's own upper waters was

[5] *Ibid.*, 124, 258. See also my article, "The Genesis of the Oregon Question," *MVHR*, XXXVI (1949-50), 583-612.

[6] *Ibid., passim;* and "Snake Country Expedition, 1824-25," *MVHR*, XXI (1934-35), 49-75.

provisioned. For the trade of the Oregon Country generally the river was required. The Governor suggested that the Oregon Country be partitioned. He called attention to the fact that on a recently published American map a boundary line had been drawn from the Rocky Mountains to the seacoast along the 49th parallel,[7] which, he thought, might be made improper use of in the future by the American government. He proposed a line that he thought would be fair to the United States and that would also answer the needs of the Company. The line began at the point where the continental divide is intersected by the 49th parallel. It fell southward along the continental divide to the place where Lewis and Clark crossed the mountains, said to be in latitude 46° 20'; thence it ran via Lewis' river (the Snake) to a junction with the Columbia, and thence, via the Columbia, to the sea. The Governor observed that this line would leave both the Columbia and Lewis' river free to be navigated by the subjects of the two nations. Perhaps he did not know that the British government had offered the United States without result a much more favorable line than this in the negotiation of 1823-24. He sent with his letter a map on which he had marked his line and the location of the Company's posts in the Oregon Country. He made the suggestion, in conclusion, that Governor Simpson was in town and would be happy to attend any appointment the foreign secretary would be pleased to make should further information respecting the Oregon Country be desired.[8]

This was the letter that stimulated Canning to propose reopening the Oregon negotiation. The endorsement he wrote on it, upon reading it, was: "This is a very important Paper. The Map which accompanied it should be carefully preserved & the whole

---

[7] Cartographers in the United States in this period commonly depicted the northern boundary of the United States as established from the Rocky Mountains to the Pacific at the line of the 49th parallel. This was done either in ignorance or in excess of cartographic patriotism. The error was pointed out by Henry S. Tanner in his *A New American Atlas*, published in Philadelphia in 1823. Special commendation was bestowed on Tanner for this scholarly achievement by Jared Sparks, who reviewed the *Atlas* in *North American Review*, XVIII (1824), 384-385.

[8] *Fur Trade and Empire*, Merk, ed., 257-260.

placed among the Papers belonging to the negotiation with the U. States. Did Mr. Addington see Gov. Simpson & take a memo. of his communication?"[9]

The meeting desired by Canning between Addington, the under-secretary of state in the Foreign Office, and Simpson was held. Its outcome was a questionnaire drawn up by Addington for Simpson to answer. The questionnaire and the answers Simpson made to it are equally revealing.

A first set of questions related to the agricultural possibilities of the Columbia valley, a matter in which Canning had an interest. It drew from Simpson an attractive picture of the lower Columbia as the seat of a future agricultural settlement. Both banks of the lower Columbia, Simpson reported, from the seaboard inland to the Cascade portage were covered with a great variety of fine, large timber. The soil of the lowlands he described as alluvial and rich and, where well located, as at Fort Vancouver, capable of producing large quantities of grain and pasturing numerous herds of cattle and hogs. The climate he described as delightfully temperate with little or no frost or snow.

A second series of questions related to the fur potentialities of the Columbia valley. Was the hunting ground immediately on the northern bank of the Columbia good? The answer Simpson gave was that immediately on the northern bank the hunting ground was nearly exhausted of furs, but that the back country was still productive and that in all the small rivers and lakes beaver was found. Simpson declared that the trade of the Columbia as a whole was still in its infancy and that the territories to the northward and southward of the river produced an equal quantity of furs.

A third series followed, concerning the country's outlets to the sea. The Columbia and the Fraser were particularly inquired about, and a comparison of the two as outlets was requested. This series went to the heart of the Oregon problem. If the Fraser was navigable it was a possible alternative to the Columbia as an outlet, and it lay wholly north of the 49th parallel. Simpson

⁹ *Ibid.*

answered these questions by affirming that the Columbia was the only navigable river he knew between the interior and the coast. It was the only certain outlet for the trade west of the mountains, comprising thirteen of the Company's trading establishments. As for the Fraser, it was impassable. Its banks, in stretches of its course, formed precipices where the towing line could not be used, and its current was so impetuous as to render navigation in certain seasons out of the question. Simpson concluded his testimony with the round statement that in his opinion "if the Navigation of the Columbia is not free to the Hudsons Bay Company, and that the Territory to the Northward of it is not secured to them, they must abandon and curtail their Trade in some parts, and probably be constrained to relinquish it on the West side of the Rocky Mountains altogether."[10]

Canning had an even more compelling reason for wishing to reopen the Oregon negotiation. He was disturbed by the agitation that was going on in Washington for a military occupation by the United States of the mouth of the Columbia. This agitation, initially the work of a few zealots in Congress, had become of graver character. In December 1824 President Monroe had formally recommended to Congress that a military post be established at the mouth of the Columbia, "or at some other point in that quarter within our acknowledged limits."[11] Within sixteen days a bill drawn by Floyd, authorizing the establishment not merely of the post but of the territory of Oregon—a territory including all the country west of the Rocky Mountains and north of the 42nd parallel, with no restriction of northern boundary—had passed the House by an overwhelming majority and had obtained a disquietingly large vote in the Senate.[12] In De-

[10] *Ibid.*, 260-266.

[11] James D. Richardson, *Messages and Papers of the Presidents,* II, 262. "Within our acknowledged limits" was a cryptic phrase, which was intended, perhaps, to mean merely the south side of the Columbia.

[12] A description of the bill by Senator Dickerson of New Jersey is in *Congressional Debates,* 18 Cong., 2 sess. (1824-25), 690. The House vote on it is in 18 Cong., 2 sess. (1824-25), *House Journal,* 68-69, 78-79.

cember 1825 Adams had repeated Monroe's recommendation
and had added the suggestion that provision be made for a public vessel to explore the whole northwest coast of the continent.[13]
His message had led to no actual legislation but had produced an
aggressive committee report—the first of two reports of the
Baylies Committee.[14]

These proceedings had been reported home regularly by the
British ministers in Washington. In March 1826 they had been
summarized, at the suggestion of Canning, by Addington, who
had been an observer of some of them at close range while he was
minister in Washington in 1824-25. A suggestion of Addington
was before Canning that a series of British papers exhibiting the
claims of England to the Oregon Country be published by Parliament as an antidote to the agitation in Congress and a warning to the American government against aggressive action.[15] The
suggestion, apparently, did not commend itself to Canning. The
proposal to reopen the Oregon negotiation was the alternative.

The proposal was accepted with eagerness by the American
government. It opened the way for bringing not only the Oregon question but other stubborn Anglo-American issues to a
settlement. The Oregon question and a sheaf of others were made
ready for negotiation. The added issues were commercial relations with the British West Indies, which involved the colonial
and navigation laws of England; the renewal of the commercial
convention of 1815, which Gallatin and Rush had once renewed
in 1818, but which was soon to expire; the northeastern boundary
issue; the question of navigation of the St. Lawrence; and the
still unsettled question of indemnification for slaves carried off
from the United States in violation of the Treaty of Ghent. In
quantity and complexity these issues formed a load more than

[13] *Messages and Papers of the Presidents*, II, 313.

[14] The first Baylies Report is printed in 19 Cong., 1 sess. (1825-26), *House
Reports*, No. 35.

[15] H. U. Addington, "Abstract of Proceedings," March 9, 1826, F.O. 5: 221;
Addington to Canning, May 2, 1826, F.O. 5: 221. See also same to same Dec.
28, 1824, British Museum, Additional Mss., 38746:69, and Vaughn to Canning,
Jan. 30, 1826, F.O. 5: 210.

an ordinary minister could carry. The resident minister of the United States in London, Rufus King, was old and unwell. The government decided to send a special plenipotentiary to join him. The obvious man for the place was Albert Gallatin.[16] He was prevailed upon to accept. When King was presently obliged by illness to resign, Gallatin was persuaded to become resident minister to England for the period necessary to bring a general negotiation to completion.

Instructions to Gallatin were prepared under the supervision of President Adams, who was more expert on Anglo-American affairs than his secretary of state, Henry Clay. On the Oregon question the instructions were that the line of the 49th parallel must be the limit of American territorial concession. It could be so announced. The only departure permitted from it was the concession to the British of the right to navigate the Columbia River and any of its branches which the line intersected from the point of intersection to the sea.[17]

These instructions displeased Gallatin. He had asked to be given some freedom, especially freedom to make again the Gulf offer he had made informally in 1818, which involved concession of a crucial area south of 49°.[18] He had wished to be permitted to enlarge that offer by the addition of the whole drainage basin of Juan de Fuca Strait. He believed that without these concessions he could reach no partition agreement with the British. He had been promised, while he was considering acceptance of the mission, that he would be permitted to write his own instructions. He reminded the President of this in letters of remonstrance against his instructions.[19] But the President was inflexible against any retreat from the line of the 49th parallel.

---

[16] Gallatin had already dealt with some of these issues as special envoy to England in the negotiation of 1818. He had an unrivalled knowledge of American finance and economy, a mind trained to cut through complex technical issues, and a European's insight into European modes of thought.

[17] Clay to Gallatin, June 19, 1826, *ASP, FR,* VI, 644-646.

[18] See my article on "The Ghost River Caledonia in the Oregon Negotiation of 1818," in *AHR,* LV (1949-50), 530-551.

[19] Gallatin to Clay, June 20, 29, 30, 1826, in Albert Gallatin, *Writings,* II, 307, 312-313, 319-320.

CHAPTER II

WELLSPRINGS OF AMERICAN POLICY

The inflexibility of the President on the issue of the 49th parallel was no mere intransigeance of an individual. It was the will of the Senate. It reflected the temper of the nation. The President made this clear to Gallatin in a later letter discussing the instructions: "One inch of ground [beyond the 49th parallel] yielded on the North-West coast . . . would be certain to meet the reprobation of the Senate."[1]

The line of the 49th parallel had been the consistent policy of American administrations ever since the Oregon Country had become an Anglo-American issue. It had been the policy of the Madison government. In the dark days of the War of 1812 Monroe had maintained it in his instructions to the peace commissioners at Ghent. In the Monroe administration Adams had defended it in two negotiations with the British—those of 1818 and 1823-24. If Adams had wished as President to retreat from that line he could not safely have done so. Retreat would have been politically disastrous.

Yet there was something paradoxical, in that day, about defending the line of the 49th parallel west of the Rockies. The whole trans-mountain region was believed, in the first quarter of the nineteenth century, to be beyond the reach of the government of the United States. The conviction of thoughtful Americans was that if this territory were acquired, it could not be permanently held. For the United States to attempt to hold and govern it would be to fly in the face of time, space, and the dearest conceptions of American democracy.

Between the western settlements of Missouri and the Pacific coast a vast barrens was believed to extend. The Great American

[1] Adams to Gallatin, March 20, 1827, *ibid.*, 367-368.

Desert was there, a land of sterility, of dust storms and aridity. In the report of the Long expedition of 1819-20, the region between the parallels of latitude 39° and 49°, and between a line 500 miles east of the Rockies and the base of the Rockies, was declared unfit for cultivation, a region not habitable by a people dependent on agriculture, an area important chiefly as a check to too great an extension of American population westward and as a protective barrier against the incursions of an enemy in that quarter. West of this waste rose the towering peaks of the continental divide, and beyond them stretched, as far as the Cascades, another desert of sand and alkali.[2]

For the crossing of this barrens only primitive means of travel were available—the horse, the ox, the canoe. No one of right mind dreamed of railroads ever ascending the heights of the Rockies or the Cascades. It was not until 1829, two years after the close of Gallatin's negotiation, that the first crude locomotive was put in motion in the United States. Steam had come to be applied to river transport but its use for ocean transport was a development of the future. The telegraph was a development yet further in the future.

The travel time of the Lewis and Clark expedition from St. Louis to the shores of the Pacific was eighteen months. That of Robert Stuart, the Astorian, on a return trip from Astoria to St. Louis in 1812-13, via the short cut of South Pass, was ten months. The sea voyage between the Pacific Northwest and the eastern seaboard by way of Cape Horn was a matter of six to eight months depending on the weather. Communication between the Northwest Coast and the eastern seaboard was often by way of a trip around the world.

The society that would be formed in the Oregon Country was

[2] The report of the Long Expedition is in *Account of An Expedition from Pittsburg to the Rocky Mountains,* Edwin James, comp. (Philadelphia, 1823); see especially volume II, 361. See also Henry M. Brackenridge, *Journal of a Voyage up the River Missouri* (Baltimore, 1815); and Robert Greenhow, *History of Oregon and California* (Boston, 1845), 323. The persistence of the desert conception of the region beyond the 100th meridian is well traced in Ralph C. Morris, "Notion of a Great American Desert East of the Rockies," *MVHR,* XIII (1926-27), 190-200.

expected to consist of a population drawn from the United States. It would be an offshoot of the United States. If it became a colony it could be governed, doubtless, from the United States. Colonies were governed from England that were even more remote. Yet, to Americans, a colonial government, permanently maintained over a people of their own kin, seemed repugnant. It would be contrary to the genius of American democratic institutions. If attempted, it would end, so it was believed, in subverting the liberties of the republic itself. The expectation and the wish of thoughtful Americans was that the society which would be formed west of the Rockies, would take the course that the American colonies had taken and that Spain's Latin American colonies had more recently taken. It would become independent.

Such a destiny was predicted and desired by Thomas Jefferson. He was, indeed, the progenitor of the idea. In one of the letters he wrote Astor regarding the future of Astoria, he declared that he looked forward with gratification to the time when people of United States origin would have spread themselves over the whole length of the Pacific West, "covering it with free and independent Americans, unconnected with us but by the ties of blood and interest, and employing like us the rights of self-government."[3] Jefferson gave that concept wide currency. He spread it by means of conversations with disciples and friends. Among the host of his disciples, who in the 1820's were persuaded that a Pacific republic, independent of the United States, would rise west of the mountains were Gallatin, Monroe, Crawford, Clay, Benton, and probably Madison.

The most vocal exponent of this concept in Congress or in the press was Thomas Hart Benton. In a speech delivered to the Senate on March 1, 1825, he admitted that the United States should have limits and that he was a limitationist. Where the northern and southern limits should be, he preferred, for the moment, not to say. They were fixed by the hand of Nature,

[3] Jefferson to Astor, May 24, 1812, Thomas Jefferson, *Writings* (Ford ed.), XI, 244.

and posterity would neither lack sense to see nor resolution to step up to them. He continued:

> Westward, we can speak without reserve, and the ridge of the Rocky Mountains may be named without offence, as presenting a convenient, natural and everlasting boundary. Along the back of this ridge, the Western limit of the republic should be drawn, and the statue of the fabled god, Terminus, should be raised upon its highest peak, never to be thrown down. In planting the seed of a new power on the coast of the Pacific ocean, it should be well understood that when strong enough to take care of itself, the new Government should separate from the mother Empire as the child separates from the parent at the age of manhood.[4]

The conviction that a new republic would come to life in the Pacific West was, however, not a policy. It was merely the setting for a policy. The policy that the government should adopt regarding the prospective infant—whether to generate it, or foster it, or remain aloof from it, or even to resist its coming—was the question. It was a question on which men widely differed. Romanticists, like Jefferson, who looked forward with gratification to the appearance of the infant, would have the United States give it fostering care and protection. Benton wished to go further. He would have the American government actually plant the germ; he would have the government occupy for that purpose the harbor at the mouth of the Columbia. Less generous or romantic persons urged that the government refrain from planting or fostering what would become a western rival. They warned that the new republic would drain the United States of capital and population; that in the fur trade of the Far West and in the commerce of the Orient it would become a national competitor.[5]

[4] *Congressional Debates*, 18 Cong., 2 sess. (1824-25), 712. The limitationists were apparently not unwilling that the United States should acquire territory provisionally beyond the Rocky Mountains in trusteeship for the future new republic.

[5] For an example of this point of view see a speech by Wood of New York on Jan. 13, 1823, *Annals of Congress*, 17 Cong., 2 sess. (1822-23), 598-601.

Monroe, as president, entertained the hope that a combination of seemingly divergent policies might be possible. In March 1824, some months prior to the message which called forth Floyd's bill, he proposed to recommend to Congress that a military post be built on the shores of the Pacific, either at the mouth of the Columbia or in Juan de Fuca Strait, as a protection to the national interests. He intended to combine with this recommendation a strong argument against the formation by the United States of any territorial settlements on that coast. He intended to give a decided expression of opinion, as part of the argument, that such settlements "would necessarily soon separate from this Union." The President read to his cabinet the draft of a message to Congress embodying these ideas.[6]

Opposition to the sending of such a message was at once expressed. It was expressed by all three cabinet members present, Adams, Calhoun, and Southard. The grounds of opposition were significant. They revealed that a new point of view regarding the destiny of the Pacific Northwest was taking its place beside the limitationist view. All the cabinet members approved the recommendation that a military post be built. But all doubted the expediency of a presidential declaration that a separation of settlements formed on the coast would necessarily soon occur. Calhoun and Adams maintained that no such separation would occur. Calhoun affirmed that "the passion for aggrandizement was the law paramount of man in society, and that there was no example in history of the disruption of a nation from itself by voluntary separation." Adams was the boldest and most extreme of those who rejected Jefferson's old theories. Accepting Calhoun's conclusions, though not his interpretation of history, he declared that "a government by federation would be found practicable upon a territory as extensive as this continent, and that the tendency of our popular sentiments was increasingly toward union."[7] The tendency of our popular sentiments, to

[6] John Quincy Adams, *Memoirs,* VI, 250-251.
[7] *Ibid.*

which he referred, was another name for nationalism. Monroe, finding his advisers unanimous against him, concluded not to send the message in that form.

Parallel to the questions whether the territory west of the mountains could be held, or should be held, in the Union, was a third: Was it worth holding? Debate on this question was going on in the press and in Congress from the time of the restoration of Astoria to the conclusion of the Oregon Treaty in 1846. The opinions ventured ran the gamut, from the rhapsodies of Benton and Floyd, according to whom the country was a Garden of Eden, to the strident judgment expressed in a New York journal that the country was fit only for the seat of a penal colony.[8] The debate is hardly worth reporting. It was a display, for the most part, of ignorance and factionalism. The ignorance was at first almost unavoidable. The country was remote; its interior was not visited by American traders; it was occupied, after the collapse of Astor's enterprise, by no great American corporation comparable to the Hudson's Bay Company, having a stake in its resources and a centralized knowledge of them. The debate is an illustration of an important fact: that in the absence of reliable information the American public and government were at a disadvantage, as compared with the British government, in the formulation of Oregon policy.

Debate was also going on in Congress and in the press over individual stakes of Oregon diplomacy. It was going on especially over the most important of all the stakes, the Columbia River. In this debate Benton, Floyd, and their followers gave free rein to imagination. They pictured the Columbia as forming, together with the Missouri, a channel of communication between the Pacific Ocean and the Mississippi River, and as connecting the Northwest Coast with St. Louis. Along this channel would flow the commerce to and from the Orient. Furs from the Oregon Country would flow to China. In return teas, silks, and spices would move to St. Louis. St. Louis would become the Venice

[8] New York *Gazette*, March 16, 1822.

of the New World. A modern Tyre would rise at the mouth of the Columbia.[9]

Realists sought to bring these flights of fancy to earth by adverting to the bar lying across the mouth of the river, the waterfalls and rapids that obstruct navigation higher up the river, and the mountains that separate the heads of navigation of the Columbia and the Missouri. They called attention to Vancouver's *Narrative*, containing Broughton's report on the bar, and the oral testimony regarding the bar of American traders having a knowledge of the Northwest Coast. They cited, also, accounts of the mountain barriers by explorers and traders who had crossed them.

In reply, the Benton-Floyd school cited John B. Prevost, the agent of the American government at the Astoria restoration, whose account of his experiences, written for the Department of State, was published in 1822. In his report he declared that the bar was less a danger than it was thought to be, that it had been crossed and recrossed without trouble by the vessel on which he had traveled, and that it could be made safe for vessels of almost any tonnage if the channel through it were marked.[10] By that report the issue of the bar was long befogged. Benton disposed of the problem of the mountain barrier between the Columbia and the Missouri by pointing to the ease with which the Lewis and Clark expedition had crossed from one river system to the other.

Another of the stakes of Oregon diplomacy, mentioned occasionally in early debates and becoming steadily more prominent later, was a deep-water harbor that would be suitable for a naval station of the United States. Such a harbor was at first identified with the mouth of the Columbia. But as the in-

---

[9] The views of Benton are set forth in repeated editorials in the St. Louis *Enquirer* of the years 1819-1821; those of Floyd are in the Floyd reports of 1821 and 1822, 16 Cong., 2 sess. (1820-21) *H. Reports*, No. 45; 17 Cong., 1 sess. (1821-22), *H. Reports*, No. 18.

[10] The Prevost report is printed in 17 Cong., 1 sess., *H. Documents* (1821-22), No. 112.

eligibility of the mouth of the river became more apparent, search for a better one turned northward, toward Juan de Fuca Strait. In March 1824 a port within the strait was mentioned as an alternative to the harbor at the mouth of the Columbia in Monroe's undelivered message, and at about the same time congressional speeches began to reveal a desire for a naval station in the strait or the Gulf of Georgia.[11] Yet it was in just this period that Gallatin was proposing to concede these waters to the British.[12]

Associated, in congressional discussion, with the need for a naval station was the need for a base for whalers. Such a base, it was argued, was required for the New England whale fisheries in the Pacific, a large and growing interest, more important to the nation even than the maritime fur trade of the Pacific Northwest. The argument for a whaling base was an attempt to link the maritime Northeast with the fur-trapping West in support of an aggressive Oregon policy.

But the attempt was without result. New England whalers in this period operated almost altogether in the South Pacific. They used as their base increasingly, after the War of 1812, the Hawaiian Islands. A port on the Oregon coast would have been far out of their course. Spokesmen for the whaling interests in Congress repeatedly pointed out that they found among

[11] J. Q. Adams, *Memoirs*, VI, 250-251. In 1822, at the time of the public discussion of the Russian ukase of 1821, William Sturgis, a Boston merchant prince and dean of fur traders on the Northwest Coast, wrote a series of letters to the *Boston Daily Advertiser*, which were brought to the notice of President Monroe. In these letters Sturgis graphically described the bar at the mouth of the Columbia and its perils. He recommended strongly that Port Discovery in the straits be selected for an American naval station (*ibid.*, VI, 429; *Boston Daily Advertiser*, Jan. 28, 31, Feb. 6, 20, 1822). See also a speech by Trimble of Kentucky, delivered in the House on Dec. 21, 1824, *Congressional Debates*, 18 Cong., 2 sess. (1824-25), 40. Harbors in the straits were preferable to the mouth of the Columbia for naval stations. But since they lacked connection by water with the interior they did not seem as desirable as the mouth of the Columbia for commercial purposes.

[12] See above, p. 9.

their constituents no interest whatever in an Oregon whaling base.[13]

This uncertainty in the executive, the press, and Congress concerning the worth and the destiny of the Oregon Country was probably absent from the mind of Adams. He seems to have considered the area of high value and to have expected it to become part of the Union. Yet he did make declarations that flatly contradicted such a view and that must be taken into consideration by the historian. In 1818, in an interview with Charles Bagot, the British minister—the interview at which Bagot announced his government's decision to restore Astoria— Adams took pains to minimize the value of the Pacific West to the United States. In giving Bagot renewed assurances regarding the mission of the "Ontario," he declared, with ironic reference to Astor's enterprise, that the government "had no thoughts of making war at present for the empire of Astoria."[14] In a letter to Rush in the same period he directed the latter to remark to Lord Castlereagh "the minuteness of the present interests, either to Great Britain or to the United States, involved in this concern; and the unwillingness, for that reason of this Government to include it among the objects of serious discussion with them."[15] In instructions drawn shortly after for the negotiation of 1818, Adams, in declining a British proposal for the arbitration by the Tsar of the two western boundary problems, wrote: "But the delineation of an unsettled boundary across the western deserts of this continent, the title to establishments on the Pacific ocean, . . . where save pretensions, there is no object to any party worth contending for—to create burdensome commissions and make solemn references to a foreign sovereign for these, appears scarcely to be necessary, if altogether justifiable."[16]

[13] See *Annals of Congress*, 17 Cong., 2 sess. (1822-23), 424, 594-595, 598, 680. See also the testimony of William Sturgis in *Boston Daily Advertiser*, Feb. 6, 1822.

[14] *Memoirs*, IV, 94; Bagot to Castlereagh, June 2, 1818, F.O. 5: 132.

[15] Adams to Rush, May 20, 1818, *ASP, FR*, IV, 854.

[16] Adams to Gallatin and Rush, July 28, 1818, *ASP, FR*, IV, 378.

On the other hand, Adams wrote exultingly in his diary on concluding in 1819 the treaty with the Spanish minister which fixed the 42nd parallel as the boundary separating Spanish and American claims in the Pacific Northwest: "The acknowledgment of a definite line of boundary to the South Sea forms a great epocha in our history. The first proposal of it in this negotiation was my own, and I trust it is now secured beyond the reach of revocation."[17] In 1845, at the height of the Oregon crisis, on learning that Polk had again offered the British the line of the 49th parallel, Adams commented in his diary that Polk should have demanded the whole of Oregon; that in the Monroe administration and in his own he had made the offer of the line of 49° under the impression that it would be rejected; that its purpose had been to preserve peace and postpone the issue until such time as the United States could maintain its full claim, by an appeal to arms, if necessary.[18]

The likelihood is that Adams' disparagements of the Oregon Country were devices of policy, a tactic of chaffering such as is often practiced by seekers of real-estate bargains. His instructions to ministers at a foreign court were, to be sure, confidential and presumably candid. But such instructions are often written with a view to being communicated. Whatever the real views of Adams, he was in this case making use, for policy purposes, of a widely held American conviction that the Oregon Country was a region without value.

Yet it is evident from the unswerving determination with which the American government defended the line of the 49th parallel west of the mountains that a national interest of major importance was believed to be at stake there. If that interest was not material, if the American public was uncertain that the Oregon Country could or should be held, if expansionism was out of bounds there, what was the nature of this interest? It was

[17] *Memoirs*, IV, 275.

[18] *Ibid.*, XII, 220-221. This recollection must be discounted as a reconstruction of old age. If postponement of the issue had been in Adams' mind solely, the compromise offer of the line of 49° would hardly have been made.

political and ideological. In the Pacific West the American public and government were groping toward a wider conception of their democratic destiny in the New World. They were seeking to eliminate Britain, and Europe in general, from that part of the Pacific West which they considered to be in the orbit of the United States. Britain and Europe were to be contained outside the United States zone. Containment was the objective which gave shape and character to the Oregon problem as soon as it emerged from the mists of the Pacific.

The struggle to contain the British—to discourage their encroachments on the territory and sphere of the United States— was an old one in the history of the republic. It began immediately after the winning of American independence, with the effort to clear the British from the Northwest Posts. It continued in the resistance made to the British project of an Indian buffer state north of the Ohio, the resistance which finally halted that project in the Treaty of Ghent. It figured in the determination of the American government to keep the British from access to the upper waters of the Mississippi. It reappeared in the Astoria issue and in the protracted negotiation over the boundary in the region between the Lake of the Woods and the Rocky Mountains. The fight for the line of the 49th parallel in the Oregon Country was merely the projection to the Pacific of an old, embittered controversy.

Other European states whose influence Americans wished to push from their Pacific sphere were Spain and Russia. Spain had rights and possessions on that coast antedating all the others. Yet she was the first to be pushed to one side. By a treaty, signed in 1819 and ratified in 1821, she withdrew to the line of the 42nd parallel and ceded her rights north of it to the United States. She was ceding rights that, in view of the virtual independence of Mexico, were hardly any more hers to cede. Russia was pushed by a treaty, concluded in 1824, to latitude 54°40′. England, therefore, in 1826, remained the sole European rival to be kept out of the United States zone.

The policy of containing England was backed by intense

national emotions. One of the emotions was pride in American republicanism and a wish to safeguard it against the encroachments of European monarchy. Another was zeal for American social democracy and contempt for the "bastard liberty"[19] of the British, with its aristocracy and its inequalities. A third was love of American liberty and the wish to keep at arm's length the monopolies, the established church, the spirit of reaction associated with Britain. A fourth emotion was traditional hatred for the British on the part of large segments of the American public. The followers of Jefferson who controlled the federal government hated the British. They could not forget British aggressions against the United States on sea and on land before and during the War of 1812. The adherents of Jackson, the opposition after 1825, equally hated the British, as they showed in the eagerness with which they came to the support of the "Old Hero" on the occasion of his execution of two British subjects in his famous raid into East Florida. Adams, more than almost any other figure in American public life, detested the British. He nursed against them a hate described by Stratford Canning as "ravenous."[20]

The concept of containment was broad enough to draw support from divergent sources of thought.[21] It drew support

[19] The term was Jefferson's (Jefferson to Astor, Nov. 9, 1813, T. Jefferson, *Writings* [Mem. Ed.], XIII, 432-434).

[20] Stratford Canning to Planta, Feb. 6, 1821, F.O. 5: 157. A softening in this anti-British feeling occurred in 1823 as a result of the recognition in the two countries that they might have a common interest in preventing interference by the Holy Alliance in Latin America. Dexter Perkins has emphasized this better feeling and has held that there was a *rapprochement* of the two governments in 1823. See his *The Monroe Doctrine, 1823-1826* (Cambridge, Mass., 1932), and *AHR*, XLII (1936-37), 155. Perkins has been challenged on this emphasis by Arthur P. Whitaker in *The United States and the Independence of Latin America, 1800-1830* (Baltimore, 1941), and by Edward H. Tatum in *The United States and Europe, 1815-1823* (Berkeley, 1936), each of whom has brought important new evidence to the problem. The improvement in feeling did not in any case extend beyond 1824.

[21] The popular appeal of this objective makes understandable the course which Congress took on the Oregon issue in the period of the 1820's. The congressional course, by any other test, seems contradictory and paradoxical.

In December 1824 a recommendation was sent to Congress by Monroe that

from Adams and other expansionists who had caught the vision of the extension of the United States to the Pacific and who saw in containment a means of keeping the Pacific Northwest open as a preserve for the American republic. It drew support equally from the limitationists of the Benton school. To them it meant keeping the Pacific Northwest open for the democracy of a new republic. The association of these ideas in Benton's mind appears in his Terminus speech of 1825. He urged in it that if the United States would plant the germ of a new republic at the mouth of the Columbia, she would "find herself indemnified for her cares and expense about the infant power . . . in the exclusion of monarchy from her [United States] border, the frustration of the hostile schemes of Great Britain, and, above all, in the erection of a new Republic, composed of her children, speaking her language, inheriting her principles, de-

the employment of a frigate be authorized for the exploration of the mouth of the Columbia "and the coast contiguous thereto." A like recommendation was made by Adams as president in the next year. The reason for these recommendations was that the waters of the coast from the Juan de Fuca Strait southward to the California boundary were less well known than those north of parallel 51. The coastal waters south of the strait had never been as much frequented by maritime fur traders as those between 51° and the Bering Sea. The southern waters contained few sea otter, the prime object of the trade, whose natural habitat was the colder water to the north. The survey of the southern shore line by Vancouver had been less thorough than that north of the straits. In 1822 William Sturgis suggested in public letters, which were brought to Monroe's notice, that a government survey of the southern shore line be made. The survey recommendation of Monroe, and later of Adams, were a result.

The attitude of Congress toward the recommendations was a test of the interest of Congress in an ultimate acquisition of the Oregon area south of 49°. The survey would have been a primary step toward acquisition, and one to which the British government could not have objected. The recommendations of the two presidents were ignored by Congress. No naval exploring expedition was despatched to the Pacific Northwest by the American government until the Charles Wilkes Expedition of the years 1838-1842.

Yet the belligerent Floyd bill, which challenged the British presence in the Oregon Country and flaunted the convention of 1818, was adopted by the House with alacrity in 1825. The bill attracted the votes of congressmen who wished their constituents to know that they supported a policy of containing the British in the Pacific Northwest. The bill won an overwhelming majority in the House and a large vote in the Senate.

voted to liberty and equality, and ready to stand by her side against the combined powers of the old world."[22]

In retrospect, the fight to contain Europe in the Pacific Northwest was an interim phase of American policy. It was a negative phase. It had appeal only while the American public was uncertain of the feasibility and value of holding the Oregon Country in the Union. It attracted to the support of the demand for the 49th parallel a national sentiment that was unanimous, however divergent in origin. It kept the Oregon issue and country open until the nation was ready to follow a more positive course. It was transmuted into expansionism as soon as the progress of invention and the growth of nationalism had given Young America an opportunity to convert the nation to a program of advance to the Pacific. In the meantime, when first openly avowed as American policy in 1823, it became a major irritant in Anglo-American relations.

[22] *Congressional Debates,* 18 Cong., 2 sess. (1824-25), 712. The reasons assigned by William Sturgis, in his influential 1822 letters to the *Boston Daily Advertiser,* for wishing the American government to take military possession of Port Discovery were much the same as those given by Benton. Sturgis wished an American military post within the straits as a means of keeping England and Russia out of that area. But he believed that no actual settlement should be made by the United States on the Pacific slope. He was persuaded that no such settlement could be permanently kept in the Union. See above, note 11.

CHAPTER III

THE NONCOLONIZATION IRRITANT

Prior to 1823 no avowal was ever made by the American government of a wish to contain Europe in the Pacific Northwest. Containment was sought behind the screen of a demand for a specific line of boundary. American administrations took the paradoxical position of insisting on a boundary at the line of the 49th parallel while persuaded that territory so won could never remain permanently within the Union. Containment sought in terms of a boundary aroused no European resentment and satisfied American feeling. If it had been sought in terms of preventing the spread of European systems of society and government in America it would have generated resentment in Europe and would, in negotiations with England, have been self-defeating.

In the instructions issued to American negotiators in the early Oregon negotiations the principle of containment of Europe remained concealed. It appeared only between the lines. In the instructions issued by Monroe in 1814 to the peace commissioners of the United States at Ghent the following language was used:

On no pretext can the British Government set up a claim to territory south of the northern boundary of the United States. It is not believed that they have any claim whatever to territory on the Pacific ocean. You will, however, be careful, should a definition of boundary be attempted, not to countenance, in any manner, or in any quarter, a pretension in the British Government to territory south of that line.[1]

In the negotiation of 1818 the language used by Adams in the instructions to Gallatin and Rush was:

The new pretension, however, of disputing our title to the settle-

[1] Monroe to the American Plenipotentiaries, March 22, 1814, *ASP, FR,* III, 731.

ment at the mouth of Columbia river, either indicates a design on their part to encroach, by new establishments of their own, upon the forty-ninth parallel of latitude, south of which they can have no valid claim upon this continent; or it manifests a jealousy of the United States—a desire to check the progress of our settlements, of which it might have been supposed that experience would, before this day, have relieved them.[2]

In actual negotiations containment was kept even more out of sight. It was screened behind a demand for needed rivers and harbors. In the negotiation of 1818 Gallatin gravely upheld the thesis of needed rivers and harbors in the Pacific Northwest though believing that all the territory there would in the end be the possession of an independent republic.

In 1823 a bolder course was taken. Containment was lifted to the surface of American policy. It was made the announced program of the United States in the Pacific Northwest. At the same time its range was vastly expanded. It was stretched to cover the whole American hemisphere. A correlative was added to territorial containment. European states were warned against any extensions of colonial systems of trade exclusion to areas they claimed on the Pacific coast. The United States government asserted that the two Americas had come to be occupied by independent nations as a result of successful revolutions, and that they were consequently no longer open to new European colonization or extensions of colonial systems of exclusive trade.

Adams stated this thesis in an instruction sent to London for Richard Rush, in connection with the Oregon problem, on July 22, 1823. He phrased it as follows:

A necessary consequence of this state of things will be, that the American continents, henceforth, will no longer be subject to *colonization*. Occupied by civilized, independent nations, they will be accessible to Europeans, and to each other, on that footing alone; and the Pacific Ocean, in every part of it, will remain open to the navigation of all nations in like manner with the Atlantic.

Incidental to the condition of national independence and sover-

[2] Adams to Gallatin and Rush, July 28, 1818, *ibid.*, IV, 375-378.

eignty, the rights of interior navigation of their rivers will belong to each of the American nations within its own territories.

The application of colonial principles of exclusion, therefore, cannot be admitted by the United States as lawful, upon any part of the Northwest Coast of America, or as belonging to any European nation. Their own settlements there, when organized as territorial Governments, will be adapted to the freedom of their own institutions, and as constitutent parts of the Union, be subject to the principles and provisions of their Constitution.[3]

Five months after this instruction was written its thesis was incorporated, in language phrased by Adams, into the December message of President Monroe to Congress.[4] It became one of the three theses in the amalgam of ideas that is known as the Monroe Doctrine, the other two being: no European intervention in the affairs of the revolted states of Latin America and no American intervention in the affairs of Europe. It is itself known as the doctrine of noncolonization. It was the brain child of Adams. It is the one element in the Monroe Doctrine which is credited by historians without dissent to the Secretary of State.

It was developed in part to defend American trade interests and rights on the coast of the Pacific Northwest. It was directed, in its trade aspects, at Russia. The Russian Tsar, in 1821, had issued an extraordinary ukase closing the waters of the Northwest Coast north of the 51st parallel to non-Russian vessels. He had forbidden non-Russian vessels to come within a distance of one hundred Italian miles of the coast.[5] The decree was an encroachment on the established rights of the United States and of England. By implication it was an assertion, also, of Russian sovereignty over the whole coast north of 51°. It collided with the territorial claims of both the United States and England. It more especially collided, in that latitude, with the maritime rights of the United States and the territorial claims of England. The American and British governments contemplated a united

[3] Adams to Rush, July 22, 1823, *ibid.*, V, 792-793.
[4] *Messages and Papers of the Presidents*, II, 217-218.
[5] The ukase is printed in *ASP, FR*, IV, 857-861.

front against Russia on this issue. Adams drew up the instruction to Rush of July 22, 1823, with this possibility in mind. On the same day that he sent off the Rush instruction he sent another of the same purport to Henry Middleton, the American minister at St. Petersburg.[6]

In March 1826, several years after the noncolonization doctrine appeared, Adams described it altogether as a principle of trade. He attributed it exclusively to the trade presumptions of the ukase of 1821. He was then President of the United States and presented this interpretation in a message to Congress in which he defended the doctrine against attacks that had been made on it by the opposition. He asserted that the doctrine rested on reasoning "equally simple and conclusive": namely, that the Americas, by virtue of having become occupied by independent states, were no longer open to extensions of colonial systems of exclusive trade.[7] This trade attribution was later taken over at its face value by historians of the doctrine and became the standard emphasis. The doctrine was explained as a policy of the "open door" for the Pacific Northwest, a program of keeping unobstructed the avenues of trade in the New World.[8]

This explanation was too simple. It did not comport well with the language of the doctrine or the facts regarding it. One important fact which it left unexplained was that the doctrine was addressed to England as well as to Russia, and was given, in the Rush instruction, its most emphatic and detailed form. With England the United States had no issue of trade exclusion in the Pacific Northwest. On the contrary the United States and Britain had a trade agreement there, the convention of joint occupation of 1818, and Adams believed that the British government might join the American in a combined front against Russia on the ukase issue.

The ascription of the doctrine so exclusively to the Russian ukase is difficult to reconcile even with the facts regarding the

[6] Adams to Middleton, July 22, 1823, *ibid.*, V, 436-437, 445.

[7] *Messages and Papers of the Presidents*, II, 334-335.

[8] See Perkins, *The Monroe Doctrine, 1823-26*, chap. i.

ukase. The ukase was issued in the late summer of 1821. It was brought to the attention of Adams in January or February of 1822. It was followed by an extended correspondence with the Russian foreign office via the American minister in St. Petersburg and the Russian minister in Washington. Adams made no use of the doctrine of noncolonization against the ukase while it was a genuine trade issue. In August 1822 Middleton notified Adams that the Russian foreign office had assured him the ukase would not be carried out. In July 1823, when the noncolonization doctrine was formulated, the ukase had long been, as a trade problem, a dead issue.[9]

Noncolonization as a principle was not single in purpose. It was double, territorial and commercial. It was mainly territorial, and incidentally commercial. It was a ban on new colonization by Europe. Its name defines its major purpose. It was a principle of territorial containment.

It was containment in extreme form. It was containment directed no longer to a modest United States sphere of influence —to territory on the Pacific coast contiguous to that of the republic—but widened to apply to a hemisphere. The American sphere of influence was conceived to be the western world. This was a stretching of concept congenial to Adams. He believed that North America, in all its length and breadth, would be absorbed some day into the United States.[10] The noncolonization doctrine seems, in his mind, to have been a measure that would keep North America open as a preserve for the republic of the United States to expand over at leisure.

Even in the case of Russia the noncolonization doctrine was largely territorial. The document in which it was explained to Middleton was entitled, "Observations on the Claim of Russia to Territorial Possessions on the Continent of North America,

[9] The documents relating to the ukase are printed in *ASP, FR,* V, 432-471; *Alaska Boundary Tribunal Proceedings,* 58 Cong., 2 sess. (1903-1904), *Sen. Documents,* No. 162, II, 31-93.

[10]*Memoirs,* VI, 250-251.

communicated with Mr. Adams's letter . . ."[11] The ascription of the doctrine so exclusively to trade and to the ukase in 1826 was a tactic of policy. In 1826 Adams had learned to his cost that the territorial emphasis of the doctrine was blocking his objectives with Canning. He was facing at that time a new Oregon negotiation with England, and was preparing to mute the territorial theme. His plenipotentiary in that negotiation was to go to the length of privately disavowing the doctrine.

The doctrine was directed, in its territorial aspects, principally at England. British containment was what was uppermost in the mind of Adams. The doctrine was given its fullest and frankest formulation in the Rush instruction. It was asserted less aggressively against Russia. In the Middleton instruction it was not even incorporated into the body of the instruction but was relegated to an accompanying document, the last of a series of ten such documents.

The challenge to England in the doctrine was given point by a proposal that accompanied it in the Rush instruction. The proposal was innocent enough on its surface but carried a sting. Rush was directed to suggest to Canning a joint occupation by three states—England, Russia, and the United States—of the Oregon Country for a period of ten years. Rush was to propose, with a view to a definitive future demarcation of boundaries, that no more British settlements be established south of the 51st parallel or north of the 55th parallel, that no more Russian settlements be made south of the 55th parallel, and no American north of the 51st. Should Britain earnestly insist on the 49th parallel, however, the United States would consent to carry that line to the sea, this being the boundary east of the Rocky Mountains. The sting in the instruction was the proposed restriction upon England north of the line of 55°. Adams was there

[11] See references cited in note 9. Adams asserted the noncolonization principle to the Russian minister in Washington orally five days before he incorporated it in the Rush and Middleton instructions. This assertion was the first appearance of the doctrine.

intervening in an area that had hitherto been assumed to be a zone of only Anglo-Russian rivalry. What Adams had in mind in this area and in this instruction has remained an historical enigma. He was reconciled to permitting the country north of 55° to go to Russia and had proposed this to Russia in July 1823. To England, however, he showed in the instruction, he was unwilling it should go.[12]

The forces which shaped and timed the noncolonization pronouncement were not crisis factors such as shaped the companion pronouncement of nonintervention in the Monroe message. On the Northwest Coast there was no crisis in 1823 to call forth such a doctrine. The Russian situation was taken merely as an occasion for giving forth the doctrine. Adams himself suggests this in the message of 1826. How little there was of emergency in the doctrine is indicated by the proposals that accompanied it in the July instructions. They amounted to an offer to leave the region north of 49° to England and to Russia, an offer followed by a treaty in 1824 which left to Russia all the area north of 54° 40' and also the exclusive trade of its territorial waters, subject only to the reservation to the United States of a ten year trading privilege. A trading post of the Russian American Company at Bodega Bay in California cannot have been the occasion of the pronouncement. It had been built as early as 1812, and Adams was not sufficiently alarmed by it to make it an issue in the Russian negotiation of 1824. With Britain there was similarly little in the way of crisis in 1823 on the Northwest Coast.

The enunciation of the noncolonization doctrine seemed to Albert Gallatin premature. It seemed so to him as late as 1846.[13] In 1848 Calhoun declared that the doctrine had appeared in

---

[12] Adams may have had in mind establishing bargaining leverage in this latitude for the United States which could be used to obtain commercial concessions for American vessels from Russia in the portion of the Northwest Coast that would be assigned to Russia. This is hinted at in Richard Rush, *Memoranda of a Residence at the Court of London* (Philadelphia, 1845), 470, and in *Alaska Boundary Tribunal Proceedings*, I, pt. 1, 28.

[13] A. Gallatin, *Letters on the Oregon Question*, 17.

the message of Monroe without any previous cabinet deliberation on it. He condemned it as having been impolitic, unclear in formulation, "broader than the fact"—which was a manner of saying that it was extreme—and that it exhibited "precipitancy and want of due reflection."[14]

The conception upon which the doctrine seems to have been predicated, that the United States would expand as a federal republic over all North America, was unrealistic and wild. Even today, in an age when travel has come to approach the speed of sound, the concept of a federal republic of the United States embracing the whole continent is as remote and extravagant as ever. In 1823 it was not merely extravagant, but inconsistent with other concepts of Adams. A United States authority, extending over an entire continent, inevitably meant, whatever it might be called, colonialism or autocracy. Both were abhorrent to Adams. In 1821, in a Fourth of July oration directed at Great Britain, which won Adams wide notice, he bitterly assailed colonialism as a system based on immorality.[15] Yet a United States, stretched to the dimensions of a continent, would inevitably have generated a new colonialism.

In 1823 Adams was a leading candidate for the succession to the presidency. He had proved himself an exceptionally energetic and able secretary of state. He was in a strategic office for the succession. He was the outstanding northern candidate, supported as such by states that had become sensitive on the slavery issue as a result of the clash over the admission of

[14] John C. Calhoun, *Works*, IV, 462. The instruction to Rush probably did not receive the careful scrutiny of Monroe. The President was of the opinion that any society formed in the Pacific Northwest would be beyond the reach of the American government and would necessarily, if formed, soon separate from the Union. He was of that opinion as late as March 1824. In the Rush instruction, however, the Adams thesis was asserted, that settlements formed on the Pacific coast, would, when organized as territorial governments, be "constituent parts of the Union" and "subject to the principles and provisions of their [United States] Constitution." See above, p. 26.

[15] John Quincy Adams, *An Address Delivered at the Request of a Committee of the Citizens of Washington: on the Occasion of Reading the Declaration of Independence, on the Fourth of July, 1821* (Washington, 1821).

Missouri into the Union. In an era of virulent factional rivalries, he was the target of attack by the adherents of every other contender for the presidency. His rivals sought to fasten on him the charge that, as a New Englander, he had consistently betrayed western interests. His great diplomatic triumph, the Adams-Onís treaty was denounced as an unnecessary sacrifice of Texas to Spain.[16] The most damaging charge hurled at him was that he had been unduly soft in dealing with England. The adherents of Clay, Floyd among them, charged, in the famous Jonathan Russell affair of 1822, that he had exhibited an undue willingness at Ghent to concede the navigation of the Mississippi River to the British—"to let the British into the heart of our country"—in exchange for the continuation to New Englanders of the fisheries liberty.[17] He was accused by Benton of having betrayed the West on the Oregon issue. Benton, on February 17, 1823, made a survey of the issue in a Senate speech which was loaded with political dynamite.[18] He read the instruction which Adams had written Gallatin and Rush in 1818, in which the New Englander had referred to the "minuteness of the present interests, either to Great Britain or to the United States, involved in this concern [Oregon]; and the unwillingness, for that reason of this Government to include it among the objects of a serious discussion with them."[19] Benton noted the fact that Prevost, the agent of the State Department who had been sent to the mouth of the Columbia in 1818 to receive the restitution of Astoria, had traveled going and coming, as a guest on a British ship of war.[20] The ominous circumstance was recalled that the convention of 1818, of which the Oregon agreement of joint

[16] Carl Schurz, *Henry Clay*, I, 162-165; *St. Louis Enquirer*, March 31, 1819.

[17] Adams, *Memoirs*, index: *Writings*, VII, 250-367; and *The Duplicate Letters, the Fisheries and the Mississippi: Documents Relating to Transactions at the Negotiation of Ghent, Collected and Published by John Quincy Adams* (Washington, 1822).

[18] *Annals of Congress*, 17 Cong., 2 sess. (1822-23), 246-251. See also *St. Louis Enquirer*, March 17, 1819.

[19] See above, p. 18.

[20] See my article, "The Genesis of the Oregon Question," *MVHR*, XXXVI (1949-50), 583-612.

occupation was part, opened with an article securing to New England fishermen the liberty of curing fish on the unsettled coasts of Newfoundland and Labrador. The joint occupation agreement itself, Benton charged, left England in virtual possession of the Oregon Country. These were charges that an aspirant to the presidency could not leave unanswered.

Adams was eager for the presidency. He had been quietly nursing the ambition throughout his secretaryship. He did not confess this freely even to himself, but his private correspondence and his diary reveal it clearly and his family was well aware of it. He watched the maneuvers and twistings of his rivals with jealousy and bitterness of soul. His comments on them in his diary were written in acid. His Puritan conscience forbade his descent into the ring with his rivals. He believed that the office seeks the man, and not the man the office. When the opportunity offered to strike successfully at his detractors, as it did in the Jonathan Russell affair, he struck with crushing and unmerciful force. He kept this issue of personal politics alive in the press until even the appetite of that politics-hungry generation was satiated. Then he followed it up with a lengthy pamphlet.[21] His private correspondence from May 1822 to April 1823 is dominated for more than a hundred pages of printed matter by this issue.[22]

Adams realized that the most damaging of the charges against him, if permitted to stick, was that he had been weak in the face of British encroachments in the West. This was a charge to which an answer could be given without a descent into the hurly-burly of politics. Instructions issued by the Department of State on important foreign issues passed with surprising promptness into public knowledge by the road of congressional calls upon the executive for documents. The challenge to England and to Russia in the July instructions and in the December message of the President would serve as a resounding answer to detractors.

[21] See the references cited in note 17.
[22] *Writings*, VII, 250-367.

The trumpet blast of noncolonization is not to be explained primarily in these political terms. It was the expression of a universal desire of the American public to contain Europe in the Pacific West. It reflected the deepest convictions of Adams, who, like Canning, his British counterpart, identified his own intense nationalism, his inordinate expansionism, and a high tone in addressing foreign governments, with the national good. The doctrine was a typical illustration of the uncertainty of Adams' judgment, an inability to sense that tactics of aggressiveness which had been used with success against Spain in 1819 would not be profitable against England, especially in an Oregon negotiation in which real British concessions would have to precede a settlement. These elements all contributed to the doctrine. But the blast and its timing cannot be fully understood, in the absence of any real crisis and in the light of the risks it created in the coming British negotiation, without a recognition of the fact that July and December 1823 were the eve of a presidential election.

The doctrine was made known to Canning gingerly and piecemeal by Rush. The injection of so explosive an issue into a negotiation sufficiently difficult in itself Rush postponed as long as possible. As a first step he prepared merely a memorandum of the tri-partite partition proposal of Adams, which he carried to a conference with Canning. He found Canning confined to bed by an attack of the gout and apparently less aggressive than usual. When the foreign secretary learned that the American boundary demand had been lifted to the 51st parallel he merely ventured the remark that it was beyond anything England had anticipated. But on Rush's departure he examined the memorandum left with him and for the first time became aware of the proposed restriction on Britain at the 55th parallel. He wrote Rush immediately:

What is here? Do I read Mr. Rush aright? The United States will agree to make no settlement north of fifty-one, on Great Britain agreeing to make none south of that line. So far all is clear. The point of contact is touched, and consequently the point of possible dispute between the United States and Great Britain; but the memorandum goes on, "or north of fifty-five"!

What can this intend? Our *northern* question is with Russia as our *southern* with the United States. But do the United States mean to travel *north* to get *between* us and Russia, and do they mean to stipulate against Great Britain, in favor of Russia, or reserve to themselves whatever Russia may not want?[23]

The answer Rush was obliged to give was "that it was even so."[24]

The noncolonization doctrine was fully disclosed to Canning only after it had been made public in the Monroe message. It seemed to him the colossal impertinence of an upstart state. It seemed an attempt to interdict a process of European colonization that was as old as the voyage of Christopher Columbus. It seemed as bizarre as the doctrines that underlay the ukase of 1821. It appeared to be a challenge to British colonization of every part of the Oregon Country and of all other unappropriated portions of North America. His rage over the doctrine was intensified by the section of the Monroe message in which the American government took upon itself singly to warn Europe against intervention in Latin America. That section of the message stole his own thunder. It asserted for the United States the role of protector of Latin America, which he was ambitious to play in the eyes of the world and in the eyes of his British constituents. His rage over these elements in the message burned in him throughout his final years as Foreign Secretary and as Prime Minister.

As a result Anglo-American issues became exacerbated. Those relating to the Pacific Northwest became impossible to settle. The project of a joint Anglo-American negotiation with Russia over the ukase issue ended in failure, and this was the prelude to the failure of the separate Anglo-American negotiation over Oregon, begun early in 1824. In the separate negotiation, the noncolonization doctrine, finally resorted to by Rush as a support to the American position in the Oregon Country, was met

---

[23] Richard Rush, *Residence at the Court of London,* 468-469.
[24] *Ibid.*

by a flat denial of its validity on the part of the British: "The British plenipotentiaries asserted, in utter denial of the above principle, that they considered the unoccupied parts of America just as much open as heretofore to colonization by Great Britain."[25] According to Rush, the anger of Canning over the noncolonization doctrine was chiefly responsible for the stalemate in which this negotiation, like the preceding one, ended.[26]

In 1826 Canning was still at white heat. His anger had become intensified by the growing agitation in Congress for the military occupation of the mouth of the Columbia. To Canning, noncolonization and the agitation were components of a single American policy of aggression. They aroused all his combative instincts.

In 1826 Adams, now president, was ready to subordinate the preaching of noncolonization to the practical necessities of negotiation. He had learned prudence from the reception accorded by Canning to his doctrine. In the instructions which he drew for the Gallatin negotiation, he permitted the doctrine quietly to recede into the shadows cast by concrete demands. He swerved "not an inch of ground" from the demand for the 49th parallel, and he made clear privately to Gallatin that he had not changed his views as to his principle.[27] But he permitted the didactics of the doctrine to be withheld. Of this

[25] *ASP, FR*, V, 563.

[26] Rush, *Residence at the Court of London*, 470-475. Canning to British Commissioners, May 31, 1824, *Some Official Correspondence of George Canning*, Edward J. Stapleton, ed., II, 76-85; Hughes to Gallatin, Dec. 10, 1826, Gallatin Papers, New York Historical Society. See also Gallatin to Clay, Dec. 20, 1826, *ASP, FR*, VI, 658-659.

[27] On March 20, 1827, the President privately wrote Gallatin: "For the causes of this present soreness of feeling we must doubtless look deeper than to the report of a committee of our House of Representatives, or to the assertion by the late President that the American continents were no more subject to future colonization from Europe. As the assertion of this principle is an attitude which the American hemisphere must assume, it is one which no European power has the right to question; and if the inference drawn from it of danger to *existing* colonies has any foundation, it can only be on the contingency of a war, which we shall by all possible means avoid . . ." (A. Gallatin, *Writings*, II, 366-367).

withholding Gallatin made full use for purposes of conciliation. He did so to a degree that might have startled Adams had he known it. At the third meeting with the British plenipotentiaries, according to a report made to Canning, Gallatin

repeated with some emphasis an observation which he had already made with respect to the denial of the right of future colonization by Europeans in any portion of the New World, of a principle which had been maintained by his predecessor (Mr. Rush) in conformity with the language of the then President of the United States, Mr. Monroe. That doctrine, Mr. Gallatin said, he had no instructions to put forward, or even touch upon. The Committee of the House of Representatives, he added, had in their report on the subject of the Columbia River, made during the last session of Congress, disclaimed the principle advanced by Mr. Monroe; that the American Government, also, had no intention of acting upon it was evident from the circumstance of their having proposed to Great Britain a certain line of boundary beyond which it was clear that the latter would have the right and power to establish whatever colonies they pleased. It could not be expected, Mr. Gallatin added, that a Government should go further than this in renouncing a doctrine once avowed by them, but we might judge of their intentions by their acts.[28]

This private disavowal by a minister of the United States of a declared policy of his government is a measure of the feeling which that policy had aroused in British foreign office circles. It registered temperatures that had to be reduced. It was a measure of the difficulty of the task which Gallatin faced in 1826.

[28] Huskisson and Addington to Canning, Dec. 7, 1826, F.O. 5:219. The Baylies report, to which Gallatin referred, contained the comment on the noncolonization project: "We do not propose to enter into the discussion of the principle asserted by Mr. Monroe, that no part of the continent of North America is now to be considered as open to European colonization. For ourselves we can only say that we are not disposed to quarrel with any nation for colonizing any portion of the American wilderness, without the limits of the United States" (19 Cong., 1 sess., *H. Reports* [1825-26], No. 213, p. 14).

CHAPTER IV

CLIMATE OF BRITISH OPINION

In England there was no public opinion comparable to the American on the Oregon question. Public opinion was latent; it was not declared. Public discussion of the question was conspicuously absent. There was no Oregon debate in Parliament at any time prior to 1840; indeed, hardly any thereafter. No parliamentary committee report on the issue ever appeared. The question was similarly unnoticed before the forties in the British press. The forces shaping Oregon policy in England were under the surface; they operated more quietly than in the United States.

Most active of the forces shaping Oregon policy was the Hudson's Bay Company after 1821. The Company was almost the only direct force. Its influence was exerted privately; it preferred to remain out of public sight. It published no reports. It discouraged publication by its employees even of narratives of their adventures in the fur trade. Its method was to influence cabinet members in strategic positions. It exerted influence especially on Canning, who, in the years from 1822 to the time of his death in 1827, very nearly determined the Oregon policy of the British government.

The influence exerted by the Company was not due to any major trade interest that it guarded in the Columbia valley. The Columbia trade of the Company, in terms of empire values, was surprisingly slight. The extent of it was indicated by Governor Simpson in response to a query presented to him in the Addington questionnaire. The query concerned the annual profits of the Company in the Columbia district and whether the profits arose principally from the northern or the southern part of the district. Simpson evaded the issue of the profits. He gave instead the somewhat more impressive figure of the gross value of the furs taken. The gross value he gave was between £30,000 and £40,000, which was divided about equally between the northern and the southern parts of the Columbia valley. This was a total less than the gross of many a Lancashire textile establishment. Simpson was careful to preface his testimony by the observation that the trade of the Columbia was yet in its infancy, which was, however, an opinion of doubtful accuracy.[1]

The explanation of the Company's influence with Canning was probably the identity of its aims and his. Its representations of facts and its formulations of policy lent support to positions he wished to take in the Cabinet regarding the building of the empire and the stimulation of British trade. In Gallatin's opinion the Company exerted a smaller influence on Oregon policy than the North West Company had once done. Gallatin expressed this view at the close of his negotiation. He did not explain the decline, but it was probably the result of the growing objection in England to all government-intrenched monopolies. Gallatin reported, however, that the Company had been and would continue to be the principal bar to a definitive settlement of the boundary. "Of the monopolizing, rapacious, and unfriendly disposition of that company," he reported to Clay, "you are well apprised."[2] One indication of its influence was the ready response Canning made to the letter of the London governor suggesting the reopening of the Oregon negotiation.

Emotional forces were important elements shaping British Oregon policy. One of them was the pride Britons felt in the Empire, in the magnitude of the Empire, in the thought that upon the Empire the sun never set. Englishmen were stirred by the very remoteness of the Northwest Coast, by the thought that in this far corner of the world there would some day rise a flourishing British colony and commerce. These were emotions that found reflection in the columns of the London *Times*. They were the spirit of Canning.

[1] *Fur Trade and Empire,* Merk, ed., 263.
[2] Gallatin to Clay, August 10, 1827, *ASP, FR,* VI, 694.

Of the same substance were British recollections of the triumph of Pitt over the Spanish in the Nootka Sound affair. To many Britons the Northwest Coast and Nootka Sound were synonymous terms. Gallatin was struck by the importance of the Nootka Sound tradition in British thinking on the Oregon issue. It was especially a factor in the thinking of Canning, who was a disciple and a political heir of Pitt.[3]

But by no means all Britons viewed the Empire with pride. Some—the philosophically minded "little Englanders"—viewed it as a liability. They believed that England had attained greatness and prosperity not by any possession of colonies, but by capacity to manufacture cheaper and better and to carry on commerce more profitably than other nations. They regarded colonies, British North America particularly, which cost more to administer than the revenue they produced, as a drain on the mother country. In 1825 John Ramsay McCulloch, the eminent Scottish statistician and economist who was a leading exponent of such views, declared in an article in the *Edinburgh Review*: "We defy any one to point out a single benefit, of any sort whatever, derived by us from the possession of Canada, and our other colonies in North America. They are productive of heavy expense to Great Britain, but of nothing else." "Every man of sense," McCulloch affirmed, "knows, that Canada must, at no distant period, be merged in the American republic."[4] Such a fate for Canada many Englishmen, including Alexander Baring, contemplated with equanimity.

"Little Englanders" believed that the Pacific Northwest would become an independent state. It would, they were sure, follow the course which the Latin American provinces of Spain and, earlier, the United States had taken. The spectacle of the dissolution, continent wide, of the Spanish empire in America profoundly affected the thinking of these men. The independence of the Latin

---

[3] *Ibid.;* Canning to British Commissioners, May 31, 1824. *Some Official Correspondence of George Canning,* II, 78.

[4] XLII (1825), 291-292. For an indignant reply to this article see *Quarterly Review,* XXXIII (1825-26), 410-429.

American states had had for its immediate effect a great en-
largement of British markets, profits, and influence in diplomacy.
The prospect that the Pacific Northwest would become independent was welcome to them for similar reasons.[5] But if the
philosophy of the "little Englanders" touched some members
of the British government it had no place in the thinking of
Canning.

Other emotional forces than the love of empire stamped themselves upon British Oregon policy. Among them was jealousy
and apprehension of the growth of the United States. Jealousy
was keen regarding the territorial growth of the United States.
The United States in 1783 had extended westward only to the
Mississippi. In 1803 it had advanced at one stride to the Rocky
Mountains. In 1812 it had declared war in order, so the English
believed, to conquer Canada. During the war it had edged into
West Florida. In 1819-1821, it had acquired East Florida and,
in addition, Spanish rights to a large part of the Northwest
Coast. Its citizens and its ambitions were flowing into Texas.
The United States was becoming the colossus of the New
World. Its population was increasing by geometric progression.
Of this increase a considerable part was drawn by immigration
from Britain.

Even greater jealousy and anxiety was felt in England regarding the sea growth of the United States, the expansion of
the American merchant marine. That development seemed
to the British a challenge to them in their traditional sphere of
supremacy. The American merchant marine had grown phe-
nomenally during the quarter century of the wars of the French
Revolution, when it was the only important neutral carrier on
the ocean. It had become, next to the British, the greatest in
existence. The alarm that its growth had caused in England
had been a major factor in producing the War of 1812. In the
period following the war, a period of intense shipping depres-

---

[5] Alexander Baring was an illustration of the "Little Englander" who believed that an independent state would rise in the Pacific Northwest. He was
a merchant prince of London.

sion and severe competition for freights, Americans were out-distancing the British. They seemed to be gaining on the British in all the commerce lanes of the world. They seemed especially to be gaining in the Pacific.

The commerce gains of the Americans in the Pacific were attributed in England to the privileges in the China trade held by the East India Company. Under an ancient charter, that company had once possessed sole rights of British trade between Britain and all the coasts and islands in the Pacific and Indian oceans. In 1813 Parliament had passed a statute which paved the way for the termination of the China monopoly. Under the statute the India trade was opened at once to independents. However, the sole and exclusive rights of British trade to and from China and the sole British rights in the tea trade to and from all places between the Strait of Magellan and the Cape of Good Hope were continued to 1834. Parliament had also provided, in the interests of the East India Company, that any British vessel clearing for a port within the Company's limits must be of a burden of at least 350 tons.[6]

The Pacific coasts of North and South America lay within the Company's limits. Furs taken on those coasts could be shipped to China only in vessels of the Company. In 1793, following the Nootka Sound affair, Parliament had somewhat eased this restriction. It had permitted independent traders to ship furs from the Northwest Coast to China in vessels which the East India Company licensed.[7] The Company felt obliged, in view of Parliament's action, to grant such licenses whenever applied for. But it required the furs so shipped to be sold in China for bills of exchange or cash. Furs could not be bartered for tea or other China produce, which meant a reduction in their sales value by 20 per cent or more. The vessels bringing the furs had to sail away empty from China or be sold. Finally, the 350-ton requirement on vessels clearing for points within the

---

[6] *British Statutes,* 53 George III, c. 155. The act provided that after 1831, on three years notice by Parliament, the China monopoly of the Company should expire.   [7] *Ibid.,* 33 George III, c. 52.

Company's limits meant the virtual exclusion of British vessels from the trade between the Northwest Coast and China since on the Northwest Coast smaller vessels were better suited to enter the bays for furs. The net effect of the Company's restrictions was to make of the Pacific what Richard Rush in 1819 described as a "void" in British independent enterprise.[8]

Into this void American enterprise sailed. At Canton, Americans developed a trade in the years between the close of the American Revolution and the early 1820's which was of greater value than that of the East India Company. In 1818 no less than 214 American vessels, according to a list offered in evidence before a committee of the British House of Lords, were absent from the United States on trading voyages to China and India.[9] American vessels not only supplied the markets of the United States, formerly the possession of the British, with all the tea, silk, and other oriental goods consumed, but those of continental Europe with nearly all their tea requirements. Americans even did the carrying from British ports to China of British manufactures, a trade from which British independents were excluded.

An outcry was raised in England against these burdens on British commerce in the Pacific. It was an outcry led by the shipping and commercial interests. Its climax came in 1820-21, when, in both houses of Parliament, committees were investigating and holding hearings on the problem.[10] In the testimony submitted to these committees the opponents of the East India Company all came to similar conclusions. British shipping was being rapidly replaced, in the commerce of the Pacific, by American. Even without the fettering restrictions of the Company, British vessels could barely meet American competition. Vessels in which the trade to the Orient was best carried, vessels of small tonnage, were more cheaply built in the United States, where timber costs and taxes were lower, than in England.

[8] Rush to Adams, April 14, 1819, State Department, England, Despatches, 23. Rush gives a graphic account, in this despatch, of the British alarm over the growth of American commerce in the Pacific.

[9] British Parliamentary Papers, 1821, VII, Document 476, pp. 88-91.

[10] See Brit. Parl. Papers, 1821, VI, Doc. 746; VII, Doc. 476.

Vessels of every tonnage were more cheaply victualed in the United States than in England. American seamen were, in general, superior in character and in enterprise to the British. They were normally permitted to operate, in the trade of the Northwest Coast, on shares with the owners. The trade to the Orient was highly profitable to Americans. Its profits equaled the cost of the entire consumption of oriental produce in the United States, as affirmed in a report made to Congress by the Lowndes committee on currency.[11] This rich trade, and indeed the Pacific, was being bestowed, the critics maintained, upon Americans by the shackles which the East India Company imposed on British commerce.

In 1820 Edward Ellice, a prominent member of Parliament and partner in the North West Company, testified before the Lord's Committee on the baneful effects exerted by the East India Company privileges on the trade between the Northwest Coast and China. He did so in terms of the experiences of his own company. He testified that his company had experimented for several years with fur shipments in its own vessels, under license from the East India Company to China. The experiment had failed because the furs could not be exchanged for tea and the vessels had been obliged to sail from China empty. The North West Company had been forced to turn to Americans to market its furs in China. The mode of operation that had been adopted was to ship British manufactures in a British vessel to the American port of Boston. At Boston the goods were delivered to the American house of Perkins and Company. They were shipped in a vessel of that company to the mouth of the Columbia. The goods were there left with the agents of the North West Company. In the same vessel, under the American flag, the North West Company's furs were taken to China. So taken, they could be bartered freely for teas or other China produce. The return cargo was sent to the United States for sale. For these services Perkins and Company were paid a per-

[11] *Ibid.*, VII, Doc. 476, p. 6. The Lowndes report is in *Annals of Congress*, 15 Cong., 2 sess. (1818-19), 791.

centage of the proceeds. The savings effected by the North West
Company, under this mode of marketing, as against the license
system of the East India Company, were declared by Ellice
to amount to 50 per cent.[12]

In reply to such critics the spokesmen of the East India Company denied that the privileges of the Company were an adverse
influence on the total of British commerce in the Orient. They
denied especially that any connection existed between the Company's privileges and such growth as had occurred in American
oriental shipping. They attributed the initial American growth
to the fact that for almost a quarter of a century Americans
had been able to take advantage of the absorption of Europe
in fighting. The postwar growth they minimized. Such postwar
growth as had occurred they explained in terms of the cheapness
of American shipbuilding, the low rate of American taxes, and
the willingness of American traders to deal in teas of inferior
quality.[13]

The trade from the Northwest Coast to China in American
vessels the East India Company spokesman declared to be of
slight extent. From statistical tables, based in part on an
American authority, Adam Seybert, they showed that in 1818-19
the value of the furs taken to China by Americans was $372,000
as compared with $7,414,000 in silver dollars and a total of all
American imports into China of $10,017,000. From other Seybert
tables they showed that the Northwest Coast trade of Americans
had been at its height in 1799-1800, and that it had since steadily
declined, with the single exception of the year 1816-17.[14]

The attitude of the British government on this issue was that
the privileges of the East India Company were an unfortunate

[12] *Brit. Parl. Papers,* 1821, VII, Doc. 476, pp. 92-100.

[13] *Ibid.,* VII. See especially the testimony of Charles Grant, a director of
the East India Company, pp. 155-195, and accompanying tables. See also
VI, Doc. 746, pp. 302-325.

[14] *Ibid.;* Adam Seybert, *Statistical Annals* (Philadelphia), 1818. The increase occurring in 1816-17 is probably a reflection of the arrangement made
between the North West Company and Perkins and Company described by
Ellice.

inheritance from the past, that they should be restricted within the narrowest limits legally possible, but that they bound the state and must be endured until they expired in 1834. This was the attitude of Canning. In 1820, when he was President of the India Board, he strongly urged the Company to relinquish some of its less used privileges in the interests of the nation, but when the Company refused to yield he accepted its decision.[15]

The Orient was to Canning, as it was to all imaginative statesmen of his day, a vast unexploited opportunity. Its fabled wealth, its teeming millions, its stores of teas, silks, and spices—all the elements that had once fired the mind of Marco Polo—were an invitation still held out to the West. The East was a golden market to which Britain would send, once the fetters of the East India Company had been broken, her surplus for exchange.

It was against such a background that the Oregon issue was projected in Canning's thinking. The issue had for Canning a setting strikingly like that which Benton and Floyd gave it in Congress, though its ending was hardly the same. The trade of the Columbia valley, still slight, would expand. The Columbia would become the seat of a flourishing British colony. Between it and the Orient and Britain would flow a world-circling commerce that would be the glory and the power of Britain. This was the vision by which the policy of Canning was shaped when he became secretary for foreign affairs in Liverpool's cabinet.[16]

British apprehensions regarding the growth of the American merchant marine were evident elsewhere than in the Orient. During the period of Gallatin's London negotiation they were evident particularly in the British West Indies. The trade of the British West Indies had once been of mutual advantage to Americans and to the islanders. Food and lumber, which could not be produced in sufficient quantity in the islands, nor obtained at low enough prices from British North America, had been

[15] Canning to Chairman of the East India Company, May 17, 1820, *Brit. Parl. Papers*, 1821, VII, Doc. 476, pp. 393-394;; and Robinson to Canning, June 7, 1820, *ibid.*, 394-399.   [16] See below, p. 61.

bought from New England. In exchange molasses had been given, for which New England afforded the best market. This exchange was desired by the island planters on as free a basis as possible. It was opposed by other empire interests, especially by the British shipping interests, which expected to have a monopoly of the carrying trade within the Empire, and by the maritime provinces of British North America, which expected to have their stake in the markets of the islands protected. After the American Revolution pressure was exerted in England to have restrictions placed on the trade of the revolted colonies with the islands. The result was that the trade was kept on a precarious basis, opened by orders in council when food short-ages developed in the islands and kept closed at other times.[17]

In 1822, under an act of Parliament, sponsored by Castlereagh and Robinson, the trade was opened to vessels of the United States on a basis approaching reciprocity. The result was that the trade and the carrying had been virtually engrossed by the Americans. In 1825 Parliament, under the leadership of William Huskisson, adopted a far-reaching series of laws covering trade and navigation in the whole empire. The series was part of Huskisson's great program of reform of the trade and naviga-tion system. By one of the laws new rates of duty were established on foreign imports into the islands. By another the trade be-tween the islands and Great Britain was restricted to British ships. By a third law an offer was made to throw open the foreign trade of all British colonies, including the islands, to any foreign countries which, having colonies, would extend similar privileges to British ships in their colonies or which, having no colonies, would extend most-favored-nation privileges to British ships. The laws were intricate. It was impossible, without authoritative explanation of them, to determine their bearing on American commerce with the islands. The American Depart-

---

[17] An admirable exposition of British policy is found in Gerald S. Graham, *Sea Power and British North America, 1783-1820,* Harvard Historical Studies, XLVI (Cambridge, Mass., 1941). The best study by an American is Vernon G. Setser, *The Commercial Reciprocity Policy of the United States* (Philadelphia, 1937).

ment of State and committees of Congress, after careful consideration of the offer contained in them, decided to attempt nothing in the form of legislation but to leave the problem to negotiation.

Gallatin was given instructions to deal with the problem. On arriving in England, he was confronted by a British order in council closing the islands to American vessels on the ground that the offer contained in the statutes of 1825 had not been acted on by the American government in time. The order in council was the work primarily of Canning and Huskisson, whose interests in the reform of the British navigation system were outweighed, where the United States was concerned, by apprehensions over the growth of the American merchant marine. Gallatin sought vainly throughout his mission in London to obtain a revocation of the order. His negotiation regarding Oregon was dogged, as it had been in 1818, by a clash over a different issue on which the British were peculiarly sensitive.

British apprehension over the growth of the American merchant marine extended to the allied problem of naval supremacy. A merchant marine is the nursery of a navy. If the American merchant marine were to equal the British, the American navy would not long remain inferior to the British. In the War of 1812 the American navy had given a good account of itself, hopelessly outnumbered though it was. In individual encounters at sea and in fleet actions on the Great Lakes it had outfought the British. Its successes had been a rude shock to the British. In any future general war the United States would be aligned, it was assumed, with France. She had been thus aligned in the two preceding wars. The prospect of such a combination, when the navy of the United States would equal England's was not attractive to the British.

In the writings and speeches of British publicists and statesmen these apprehensions were a recurring theme. They began to appear as early as the Napoleonic wars. In 1805 they appeared in the widely read and widely influential pamphlet of James Stephen, *War in Disguise; or, The Frauds of the Neutral Flags.*

This pamphlet, written to the thesis that the ostensibly neutral commerce carried between the West Indies and continental Europe was actually a contraband trade and a vital service to Napoleon, gave warning to the British public that the expanded marine of the United States, which was a "vast excrescence" on the natural body of the American marine, was one that "in various quarters, is peculiarly likely to displace, by its extended dimensions, the maritime interests of England."[18]

In the period of the 1820's such views were privately or publicly expressed by the two members of the British government who were the most intimately concerned with the Oregon negotiation, Canning and Huskisson. They were expressed in 1824 by Canning with great clarity in a memorandum prepared for the members of the British goverment on the question of the revolted new states of Latin America:

Lastly: We have spoken of the United States of North America as our rivals in commerce and influence with the New States; but there is another and more formidable light in which they should be viewed.

The great and favourite object of the policy of this country for more than four centuries has been to foster and encourage our navigation, as the sure basis of our maritime power. In this branch of national industry the people of the United States are become more formidable rivals to us than any nation which has ever yet existed; more so even than the Dutch, whose rivalry in this respect occasioned several successive wars between the two countries.

The views and policy of the North Americans seem mainly directed towards supplanting us in navigation in every quarter of the globe, but more particularly in the seas contiguous to America.

Let us recollect that as their commercial marine is augmented their military marine must proportionately increase. And it cannot be doubted that if we provoke the New States of America to give a decided preference in their ports to the people of the United States over ourselves, the navigation of these extensive dominions will be lost to us and will in a great measure be transferred to our rivals.

[18] James Stephen, *War in Disguise; or, The Frauds of the Neutral Flags* (London, 1805), 135.

Let us remember, then, that peace, however desirable, and however cherished by us, cannot last for ever. Sooner or later we shall probably have to contend with the combined maritime power of France and of the United States. The disposition of the New States is at present highly favourable to England. If we take advantage of that disposition, we may establish through our influence with them a fair counterpoise to that combined maritime power.[19]

Similar views were given public expression by Huskisson in a widely noticed speech in Parliament in May 1826—the speech which proved to be the forecast of the order in council closing the British West Indies to American vessels. The United States, Huskisson declared, is England's most formidable rival "in commerce, in navigation, in naval power, and maritime pretensions." It had obtained an unfair and unwise preference in the West Indian Trade Act of 1822.

Upon what principle of fairness, upon what principle of sound policy, were we to continue this preference exclusively to a power, towards which, God knows, I entertain no feeling of hostility—far from it; but, when I am speaking of that nation in a British House of Commons, it is not improper to say, that in matters of navigation and naval power, there exists, towards us, a spirit of rivalry in the United States; a spirit of which I do not complain, but which incline every Englishman to doubt the wisdom of any measure, tending to encourage the growth of the commercial marine of America, by giving to it privileges greater than are permitted to the shipping of other states—states less jealous of our maritime ascendancy in time of war, and, at all times, confining their views upon the ocean to the industrious employment of their sea-faring people, without looking to the ulterior object of one day disputing with us the dominion of that ocean.[20]

Not merely jealousy but a general ill will was nursed by the

---

[19] Canning Memorandum, Nov. 30, 1824, Wellington, *Despatches, Correspondence, and Memoranda,* Continuation (London, 1867), II, 358.

[20] *Hansard's,* 2nd ser. XV (1826), 1182. Another statement by Huskisson of the same tenor is found in *ibid.,* XVII (1827), 646-647.

governing classes of England against the United States. The ill will was in part a residue of the bitterness evoked by the War of 1812. But it was more deep-seated. The United States was regarded by the British governing classes as a rebellious and ungrateful child that had twice, in unnatural alliance with a traditional foe, made war on its parent. Its republican form of government was an affront. Its democratic caste of society was a menace. Its very successes, broadcast by the Radicals in the opposition, seemed to threaten the established order in England.

The press of upper class society gave unmistakable evidence of this ill will. The London *Times,* the Tory press, and the conservative Whig press, were all hostile to the United States. The *Times,* the most powerful of British journals, was outstandingly hostile. It exhibited this feeling in a consistent high-lighting of the clashes that occurred between the two countries, and in a steady, carping criticism of things American. In 1818 it sought to stir up an exhausted people to a new war pitch over Jackson's raid into East Florida and his execution of Arbuthnot and Ambrister. It kept that issue alive throughout the Anglo-American negotiation of 1818 and well into 1819. It denounced as stupidities and as weakness any concessions Castlereagh made to the United States. In discussing things and persons American its habit was to refer to them sneeringly as "republican," which, in its columns, was a term of reproach. It demanded that the navigation policy of England be based on the assumption that the United States was a rival to England in peace and a likely enemy again in war.[21] It regarded British subjects who emigrated to the United States, if of the better class, as guilty of the crime of ingratitude to their country; if of the class described by Morris Birkbeck as having settled in Illinois, it dismissed them as a "bad set," whom it was a happiness to have got quit of, though it was the government's duty to prevent others from following their example. It represented American society as a mixture of boorishness and vulgarity. The tone it maintained toward the United States was

[21] *The Times,* May 14, 1818.

a lofty superiority and the criticisms it offered were poisoned by sarcasm and the barbed remark.[22]

Yet society in England was far from unanimous in such hostility to the United States. The commercial interests in England, especially those favoring freer British navigation and trade laws, were, in general, well disposed toward the American republic. Liverpool, the chief center of British-American trade, was a traditional center of pro-Americanism. In the manufacturing cities that relied on the United States for markets and raw materials there was friendly understanding. Individuals in every British party and class were tolerant toward the United States. Alexander Baring, a Tory of the liberal wing, was an old advocate of Anglo-American reconciliation. In a pamphlet entitled *An Inquiry into the Causes and Consequences of the Orders in Council*, published in 1808 as a reply to Stephen's *War in Disguise,* he urged that the success and prosperity of the United States ought to be welcomed in England, that three-fourths of the proceeds of the sale of American produce on the continent of Europe was paid ultimately to England in the purchase of British manufactures.[23] Brougham, a champion of the United States in the fight over the orders in council prior to the War of 1812, continued to be after the war a consistent advocate of Anglo-American reconciliation. Castlereagh, a high Tory, sought quietly to improve Anglo-American relations.

Even the *Times* occasionally relented in its anti-Americanism. In 1818 it printed a protest from one of its readers against its editorial thesis that America was the rival of England in peace and might be again an enemy in war. This was the protest:

It is somewhat difficult to perceive how that nation should be our enemy in peace which, in its habits, its laws, its institutions, and its language, most resembles our own, and which, owing to the influence of all these reasons, is our best and most extensive customer ... Consider but for a moment the relative positions of the two countries, and observe the raw material she affords for us to work up,

[22] This characterization rests on an examination of the London *Times* for the years 1818-1828.

[23] See especially p. 162 of the pamphlet.

and recollect how the industry of our people is supported by her demand for manufactured articles of every description. Ask Staffordshire, and the county palatine of Lancaster; ask Birmingham; nay, ask London herself, what they experienced when that valuable market was interrupted; and is there not every reason for union, and none for quarrel?[24]

An especially vigorous friendliness toward the United States was maintained in the 1820's by a small group in British politics, the Radical Whigs. This group not merely defended, it lauded the United States. It held up democratic America as an example for Parliament to follow. In democratic America, it pointed out, stability and order were maintained without repressive "Six Acts"; the franchise was reformed; government was economical; taxes were low; the masses were spared the burdens of sinecures, extravagance, and inefficiency; religious equality was assured to Catholics and every other religious group; commerce was unhampered by trade or navigation monopolies; a general prosperity prevailed in contrast to the dislocation and misery prevalent in England during much of the postwar period.[25]

Such views the Radicals carried to the public in the columns of the crusading London daily, the *Morning Chronicle*. They spread them, also, in such weekly or provincial journals as the *Examiner*, the *Manchester Guardian*, and the *Scotsman* of Edinburgh. The *Edinburgh Review*, the leading Whig quarterly, exhibited such leanings on occasion. The political figure from whom the Radicals took their inspiration was Charles James Fox, the Whig, who throughout his life had been a champion of Anglo-American reconciliation.

But the Radicals were a minority and a discredited one. In 1826 the prevailing disposition of the British public and government was unfriendliness toward the United States. Gallatin believed the unfriendliness greater than it had been at the close of the

[24] *The Times*, May 22, 1818.

[25] This characterization is based on an examination of the *Morning Chronicle* from 1818 to 1828. I have also examined the *Edinburgh Review* and a broken set of the *Scotsman* for this period.

War of 1812. He wrote Clay shortly after his arrival in London:

There is certainly an alteration in the disposition of this Government towards the United States since the year 1818, when I was last here. Lord Castlereagh and Mr. Robinson had it more at heart to cherish friendly relations than Mr. Canning and Mr. Huskisson. The difference may however be in the times rather than in the men. Treated in general with considerable arrogance till the last war, with great attention, if not respect during the years that followed it, the United States are now an object of jealousy and a policy founded on that feeling, has been avowed.[26]

In October 1826, shortly before the opening of his negotiation, Gallatin wrote this private warning to the President:

Although all my faculties are exerted . . . in trying to accommodate differences and to remove causes of rupture, it is impossible for me not to see and feel the temper that prevails here towards us. It is perceptible in every quarter and on every occasion, quite changed from what it was in 1815-21; nearly as bad as before the last war, only they hate more and despise less, though they still affect to conceal hatred under the appearance of contempt. I would not say this to any but to you and your confidential advisers, and I say it not in order to excite corresponding feelings, but because I think that we must look forward and make those gradual preparations which will make us ready for any emergency, and which may be sufficient to preserve us from the apprehended danger.[27]

In April, 1827, near the end of his mission, Gallatin again wrote:

I do not believe that there is a single question between us in which the Ministers will not be supported by the public opinion of the country in taking rank ground against us. Our dependence for friendly arrangements rests solely on the superior sense of the Ministers.[28]

[26] Gallatin to Clay, Sept. 22, 1826, Gallatin Papers, N.Y.H.S. Mission to England, May 3–Dec. 19, 1826.

[27] Henry Adams, *Life of Albert Gallatin* (Philadelphia, 1879), 621.

[28] Gallatin to Clay, April 28, 1827, Gallatin, *Writings*, II, 371-372.

CHAPTER V

THE BRITISH CABINET
AND THE OREGON ISSUE

The ministers in the British Cabinet upon whose "superior sense" Gallatin was obliged to depend in the negotiation of 1826-27 were Canning and Huskisson. They were the members of the Cabinet with whom he had direct contact. They were hardly a safe dependence for any American seeking friendly arrangements from Britain. Canning had been an obstacle to such arrangements for years. In the critical period, 1807-1809, when the United States was being subjected to the injuries and indignities from which it finally took refuge in war, he occupied the Foreign Office. His was the spirit which appeared in the famous November orders of 1807, the orders that, together with impressment, were the grievances which eventually drove the United States to war; his was the reluctance to make amends for the outrage of the Leopard-Chesapeake affair; and his was the disavowal of the Erskine agreement, which might have preserved the peace, a disavowal which he accompanied with the insulting charge that the American government had deliberately overreached Erskine.

In his second term as foreign minister, from 1822 to 1827, Canning was as implacable against the United States as in the first. He was hot with resentment over the Monroe message of December 1823; he was annoyed by the agitation in Congress over the Oregon issue; he was distrustful of American purposes in Cuba. He detested the republicanism of the United States; he was utterly and openly contemptuous of its democracy; he thought its government tricky. His mood in dealing with the American government is indicated in a note he sent Liverpool in 1825, after an interview with the aged Rufus King regarding the future of Cuba:

> I set him right upon these points; on which, if his Government blunder as sincerely as he appears to do, there is perhaps no harm done beyond the loss of time, but if—as the suspicion sometimes comes across me—this bonhomie is affected by the U.S.G. for the express purpose of being enabled to cry out and take a new line on the disappointment of their groundless expectations, why then the Yankees may be just the rogues that we have always hitherto taken them to be, but which I was willing to hope they might have resolved to be no longer.[1]

In any territorial issue in which Britain was concerned Canning was a true disciple of Pitt, an intense nationalist and imperialist. At his death the London *Times,* which was his devoted admirer in his later years, eulogized him "as an eloquent expounder and advocate of that policy which fixed a lever on every foreign soil whereby to raise the British empire to honour and prosperity."[2] The Oregon Country was soil that he believed would raise the British Empire to honor and prosperity, and the Hudson's Bay Company was the lever by which he hoped to do it.

Huskisson was a personal and political follower of Canning. He owed his admission into the Cabinet to Canning's influence. He shared Canning's jealousy of the maritime growth of the United States. He was not otherwise, however, in the opinion of Gallatin, hostile to the United States.[3] On the Oregon issue he seemed to Gallatin to hold temperate views.

The Cabinet, in the spring of 1826, when renewed discussions of the Oregon question began, was the same Tory body that had been in office in the two earlier Oregon negotiations. It had been in power since the beginning of the War of 1812 and, with growing age, had become increasingly inharmonious. Until

---

[1] Canning to Liverpool, August 6, 1825, *Some Official Correspondence of George Canning,* I, 283.
[2] *The Times,* Oct. 16, 1827.
[3] Gallatin to Clay, August 14, 1827, Gallatin, *Writings,* II, 382-383.

the spring of 1827 it was held together by the tact and character of its leader, a moderate, Lord Liverpool. It consisted of three groups, a nucleus of ultra Tories and high churchmen, a moderate group, and a Canning element comprising, chiefly, Canning and Huskisson. The ultra Tories distrusted and disliked Canning. They did so largely on personal grounds, though also on account of his advocacy of Catholic emancipation. They remembered, and did not forgive, the intrigue he had earlier carried on in the Cabinet against Castlereagh, ending in a duel. They considered him underhanded, an adventurer in politics, an insincere rhetorician, a man possessed of "talents without character."[4] So deep was their distrust of him that when, in the spring of 1827, Liverpool was obliged by the collapse of his health to resign and the King invited Canning to head a new cabinet, they refused to serve under him, and Canning was driven into forming a government in alliance with the Whigs.[5]

As soon as the Cabinet began its discussion of the Oregon issue a division appeared in its ranks. The division was occasioned by a suggestion made by Liverpool that the old American proposal of the 49th parallel be given reconsideration.[6] How the members divided and how close the division was cannot be ascertained. All that is known is that Liverpool, who usually stood with Canning, was ranged on one side and that Canning was on the other. The division was evidently close, for it remained long unresolved and eventually had to be compromised. In the meantime Canning carried on a persistent campaign of propaganda within the Cabinet to turn Liverpool and his abettors away from any thought of new concessions to the United States.

Canning's initial step was to order Addington to prepare a memorandum evaluating the claims of England and the United States to the Oregon Country. The order was given

[4] *Hansard's,* new series, V (1821), 426.

[5] *The Greville Memoirs,* 1814-1860 (London, 1938), I, 170-177.

[6] Canning to Liverpool, May 17, June 11, 1826, *Some Official Correspondence of George Canning,* II, 55, 58.

shortly after Canning made his proposal of a new negotiation to the American minister in London. The Addington memorandum, when presented on May 10, proved less an evaluation of claims than a partisan defence of that of England. It was reckless in assertion and calculated to mislead rather than instruct uninformed readers. It flatly asserted that Francis Drake, the first British mariner on the Northwest Coast, had explored the entire coast from latitude 37° to 48°, though the fact that Drake had sailed no farther northward than latitude 42° or 43° was already well known to the scholarly world. The memorandum boldly questioned Robert Gray's discovery of the Columbia. It dismissed the Lewis and Clark expedition with a mention of its name. It refurbished Canning's shallow thesis, developed in 1824, that the United States had weakened, not strengthened, its title to the Oregon Country by acquiring the title of Spain and that the two titles necessarily invalidated each other. It resurrected the theory that Astoria had been purchased, not captured, by the British during the War of 1812 and that the claim of the United States to its restitution should have been resisted.[7] Addington was a protégé of Canning. His work was a complete vindication of the position his chief had hitherto taken on the Oregon question, and wished to take again.

The memorandum was promptly submitted by Canning to Liverpool. Copies of it were distributed to the members of the Cabinet together with the printed papers of the preceding negotiations. In a covering letter Canning outdid Addington. He flatly denied what Addington merely questioned: that Gray had discovered the mouth of the Columbia. He declared in a concluding sentence that he did not know how to contemplate surrendering England's claims.[8]

Liverpool was unconvinced. He asked for further information. The two questions on which he wished more data were:

1st. What is the *value* of the trade carried on upon the North West Coast of America, and from thence through the interior?

[7] Memorandum of H. U. Addington, May 10, 1826, *ibid.*, II, 110-115.
[8] Canning to Liverpool, May 17, 1826, *ibid.*, II, 55.

2nd. Would the amended Projet of the United States (viz. the 49 Degree of Lat.) afford us any facilities as to outlet for our Communications by Nootka and other ports, and how far would such communications be less advantageous than those through the Columbia?

I should think Huskisson might be able to furnish *full* information on the *first,* and to *procure* some on the *last.* We must naturally expect that questions will be put during the discussion on both these points.[9]

The first of these inquiries was a pointed one. Liverpool knew, evidently, that the value of the trade of the disputed Oregon area would be shown by statistical data to be slight. Canning's response, in his reply to Liverpool, was to anticipate the data. He wrote:

But it is not from what our trade is now, that the question is to be estimated. It is when China shall be open to English as well as American commerce that the real value of settlements on the northwest coast of America will become apparent.[10]

A fortnight later Canning had the information that Liverpool desired ready to distribute to the Cabinet. It consisted of the letter that the Governor of the Hudson's Bay Company had sent Canning the preceding December; also Addington's questionnaire to Simpson, and Simpson's replies to it.[11] These Hudson's Bay Company materials were depositions for Canning in that they stressed the indispensability of the Columbia River as a channel of communication to the sea.

A long covering letter was sent with these documents by Canning which is highly significant. It not only pointed out the importance of the Hudson's Bay Company material but added powerful emotional arguments against the cession of the north side of the Columbia to the United States. Canning re-

[9] Liverpool to Canning, June 23, 1826, British Museum, Add. Mss., 38748:45 [Huskisson Mss.].

[10] Canning to Liverpool, June 24, 1826, *Some Official Correspondence of George Canning,* II, 62.

[11] The list of papers distributed is given in the Peel Mss., British Museum, Add. Mss., 40611:117.

ferred to the "blunder" the Cabinet had made while Castlereagh was in office in returning Astoria to the United States. This was an appeal to the fears of Liverpool, who had been Prime Minister at the time. Canning asked Liverpool to observe that the restoration had been determined on by the Cabinet

not only with the full knowledge that the Yankees have sent a ship of war to take possession of the settlement, without a shadow of right thereto, but that this fact, (the preparation of the Yankees to invade and wrest from our N.W. Cy. a settlement theirs by purchase) is put forward as a motive for surrendering it under a forced construction of the Treaty of Ghent: and then think what a task it will be to justify this transaction to Parlt., if upon this transaction we rest our justification for abandoning the whole N.W. Coast of America to the Yankees. I feel the shame of such a statement burning upon my face by anticipation.

Yet, Canning went on to say, withdrawal from Astoria had not been, after all, ill policy:

It [Astoria] lies on the south side of the Columbia, to which we are not unwilling to abjure all claim, keeping the north to ourselves, staking the midstream as our boundary. The cession of Astoria was therefore in furtherance of our present proposition. It now makes our present ground stronger by showing how willingly we departed from that part of it which we thought untenable.

But this is only true, if we maintain our present ground immovably. If we retreat from that, the cession of Astoria will have been but the first symptom of weakness, the first of a series of compliances with encroachments which, if not resisted, will grow upon success. There are two points—one of a political, the other of a commercial character—which I anxiously desire you to bear in mind in the discussion of this question.

1st. That the ambitious and overbearing views of the States are becoming daily more developed, and better understood in this country.

2nd. That the trade between the Eastern and Western Hemispheres, direct across the Pacific, is the trade of the world most susceptible of rapid augmentation and improvement. Between China and Mexico, it is now going on largely. Morier has brought me some specimens of China manufactures imported into Mexico, which vie with what we get through India in England.

We cannot yet enter into this trade, on account of the monopoly of the E.I. Cy. But ten years hence that monopoly will cease; and though at that period neither you nor I shall be where we are to answer for our deeds, I should not like to leave my name affixed to an instrument by which England would have foregone the advantages of an immense direct intercourse between China and what may be, if we resolve not to yield them up, her boundless establishments on the N.W. Coast of America.[12]

The concluding portion of Canning's letter unmasked a strange and unexpected element of strength in his position. It presented evidence straight from the enemy's camp of the soundness of his strategy. A confidential communication had been received by Canning divulging the important information that Gallatin was dissatisfied with his Oregon instructions. The message had come while Gallatin was still in America. It must have moved across the Atlantic with the speed of a diplomatist's mail pouch. The sender's name Canning withheld in transmitting the document to his chief. He may even have removed the signature at the wish of the sender. He referred to the document in forwarding it merely as "paper No. 1."

Who the sender was and how the information he gave was obtained are problems which cannot with certainty be solved. Neither "paper No. 1" nor an accompanying "paper No. 2," referred to below, have survived in the collected correspondence of Canning or Liverpool. The only clue Canning's letter gives is that the person who was the source of the information was known to Gallatin and was expected to be able to send warning back to Gallatin to get his instructions liberalized.

Though a definitive answer to the mystery cannot be given, it is possible, by piecing together scraps of scattered information to construct at least a conjecture. In the early summer of 1826 a letter was written to Sir Charles Bagot by an American, Christo-

---

[12] Canning to Liverpool, July 7, 1826, *Some Official Correspondence of George Canning*, II, 72-74.

pher Hughes, which is known to have contained the news of
Gallatin's appointment to the London mission, and in all probability carried also the information regarding his dissatisfaction
with his instructions. Sir Charles Bagot was then British ambas-
sador at The Hague. He had been elevated to the knighthood
for his earlier services as minister plenipotentiary to Washington.
He was a member of the ruling aristocracy of England, closely
connected by marriage with the Duke of Wellington. He was
a protégé of Canning, with whom he was in frequent familiar
correspondence.

His informant, Christopher Hughes, was American chargé
d'affaires in Brussels. He was well known to Gallatin, having
served while a youth as one of the secretaries to the American
commissioners at the Ghent peace conference. He had once been
a neighbor of the Gallatins in Baltimore. He was the son-in-law
of Senator Samuel Smith of Maryland. He was thus related to
Robert Smith, brother to Samuel, once secretary of state of the
United States. Hughes was a young man of social rather than
intellectual distinction, widely known in European diplomatic
circles for his family connections, his social graces and his prow-
ess as a punster. Such of his letters as have survived, private and
public, reveal a person gossipy and rambling of mind rather than
penetrating. He was vain and eager to exhibit the access he had
to high sources of information in Washington. He was in frequent private correspondence with Sir Charles Bagot, to whom
he signed himself under his nickname, "Uncle Sam." Like his
Baltimore connections he was an exponent of Anglo-American
reconciliation. He saw in Sir Charles Bagot the shining exemplar
of that policy. He was partial also to Canning, the great man,
who in 1823, while momentarily pressing the project of a joint
Anglo-American front against the Holy Alliance, had dazzled
him, as he was passing through England, with special attentions.

The transmission to Hughes from Washington of the information regarding Gallatin's instructions was probably via Senator
Smith. In the late spring of 1826 Gallatin was in Washington
conferring with Clay and Adams regarding his instructions. A

meeting occurred at that time between him and Senator Smith. The meeting was probably at the request of the Senator who had a special interest in one of the items on Gallatin's agenda, the problem of the American trade to the British West Indies. Smith had once been a wealthy merchant in the West Indies trade. He was a power in Senate politics, a forceful debater, president *pro tempore* repeatedly of the Senate, a general who had served with some distinction in the War of 1812. He was, however, an intriguer, given to cabal and to methods of indirection. He was unfriendly to the Adams administration and was eager to embarrass it politically. Gallatin had much reason to be wary of the Smith family, but because of the Senator's position and his special concern with some parts of the approaching mission, seems to have talked to him rather freely regarding the probable length of term of his mission and his disappointment over his instructions. A part of this confidence Smith at once betrayed by causing an unsigned communication to be sent to a newspaper hostile to the administration—the Richmond *Enquirer*—regarding the term of the mission with a view to embarrassing the administration. It was probably Smith, or some member of his family who wrote Christopher Hughes the news of the mission and the fact of Gallatin's disappointment over his instructions.[13]

Hughes may have hoped, in passing this information on to Bagot, that by exhibiting the conciliatory temper in which Gallatin was embarking on the mission, he would advance the cause of Anglo-American reconciliation. The use Canning made of the information to shape the thinking of Liverpool is best described in his own words:

At the same time that I press upon you the danger of concession,

[13] This account is based on the following sources: Hughes to Mrs. Gallatin, Nov. 14, 1826, N.Y.H.S., Clay to Gallatin, June 21, 1826, and Feb. 24, 1827, *ibid.*, Canning to Liverpool, July 7, 1826, *Some Official Correspondence of George Canning*, II, 74-75; Hughes Papers, Library of Congress; *George Canning and His Friends*, Captain Josceline Bagot, ed., II, 199, 284-287, 296-301, 314; *Congressional Debates*, 19 Cong., 2 sess. (1826-27), 402-418; Richmond *Enquirer*, June 9, 1826. The editor of the Richmond *Enquirer* was Thomas Ritchie, bitter political foe of Clay and Adams.

and the benefits of holding out on this question, it is a satisfaction to be able to present to you some prospect of more facility in the negotiation than probably you venture to expect, or than I expected before yesterday, when the enclosed paper No. 1 fell into my hands.

That paper was not wanted to make me feel assured either that our case is good, or that we have an interest of the deepest importance and heaviest responsibility in maintaining it. But I derive from it a hope which I had not before—that the goodness of our case is felt in the quarter in which it is most useful that it should be felt; and I have thought it advisable in that hope to let it be understood, that we are impressed with the duty of maintaining it. Hence the other enclosure, No. 2, which commits nobody but me, but which may prepare the person for whose warning it is written, either to obtain a modification of the instruction, which he may already have received from his Gov't., before he sails, or to prepare them for expecting to be called upon to modify it hereafter.[14]

Shortly after posting these materials Canning received a printed document on the Oregon question through the regular diplomatic channels from Washington. The document was the Second Report of the Baylies Committee of the House of Representatives. It was a thoroughgoing examination of the British claim to the Oregon area, especially of the claim derived from the voyage of Sir Francis Drake. From British sources it demonstrated that Drake could not have sailed higher than latitude 42° or 43° on the coast. It defended the claims of the United States and Spain and, in its concluding pages, charged Britain with inordinate imperialist ambition and uttered a half defiance of England on the issue of the Northwest Coast. Its tone was such as a committee of Congress, with its eye fixed on constituents, was likely at that time to indulge in.[15] The report infuriated Canning. He declared it was "almost tantamount to a declaration of War" against England. He refused to be persuaded that committee reports of Congress do not, any more than speeches

[14] Canning to Liverpool, July 7, 1826, *Some Official Correspondence of George Canning*, II, 74-75. No copy of "paper No. 2" could be found in the Bagot Mss. in the possession of the Bagot family.

[15] This report is printed in 19 Cong., 1 sess., *H. Reports* (1825-26), No. 213.

delivered on the floor of Congress, reflect the views of the executive. He made the document the occasion for pressing to adoption the order in council closing the British West Indies to American vessels, as Gallatin was afterwards informed.[16] A more immediate use he made of it was to send it to Liverpool with the note:

I cannot forbear selecting the enclosed despatch of Mr. Vaughan's from a mass which I received last night, and requesting your attention to it and its enclosure. After such language as that of the committee of the H. of Representatives it is impossible to suppose that we can tide over the Columbia, or can make to ourselves the illusion that there is any other alternative than either to maintain our claims or to yield them with our eyes wide open.[17]

Liverpool was silenced at last. Canning was able in November 1826, in drawing up the instructions for the negotiation with Gallatin, to write that the government had not changed its position on the Oregon issue since 1824,[18] when it had stood immovable at the Columbia River. Liverpool had been won over, perhaps, by the testimony of the Hudson's Bay Company that the river was indispensable to it; or he might have been angered by the Baylies report, or he might merely have preferred to avoid a clash with his headstrong colleague.

The lines of the negotiation were now drawn. The Americans were intrenched at the 49th parallel. The British had staked their claim at the midstream of the Columbia. Both were prepared to stand fast. This was not a favorable prospect for the success of the negotiation.

[16] Gallatin to Clay, Nov. 27, 1826, State Department, England, Despatches, XXXIII.
[17] Canning to Liverpool, July 14, 1826, *Some Official Correspondence of George Canning,* II, 115.
[18] Canning to Huskisson and Addington, Nov. 10, 1826, F.O. 5: 219.

CHAPTER VI

THE NEGOTIATION: THE BOUNDARY

The plenipotentiaries chosen to deal with Gallatin were Huskisson and Addington. Huskisson was chosen for his expertness in the commercial phases of the negotiation. He had, in 1823-24, dealt with Rush on these issues. Addington was a specialist on the boundary problems. He was the voice of Canning in the negotiation. On all topics, as Gallatin later observed, he was "extremely difficult."[1]

The conference opened on November 15, 1826. It promptly placed the Oregon issue at the head of its agenda. The British plenipotentiaries asked Gallatin to report upon a proposal which their government had made to Rush in 1824 and which Rush had taken for submission to the American government—the proposal that the boundary be the 49th parallel from the Rockies to the Columbia, and thence be the channel of the Columbia to the sea. Gallatin reported that this proposal had been declined by the American government. He then submitted his counterproposal. It was the old American offer—the undeviating line of the 49th parallel. As tactfully as possible Gallatin gave notice that on this line his government would insist. At the same time he offered the important new concession permitted by his instructions. The United States would make the navigation of the Columbia and any of its tributaries intersected by the 49th parallel perpetually free to British subjects from the point of intersection to the ocean, provided the waters below the point of intersection should prove on examination to be "navigable by boats." This proposal was taken by the British, without comment, for reference to their government.[2]

A discussion of claims took place at the second session and

[1] Gallatin to Clay, July 29, 1827, *ASP, FR*, VI, 684.
[2] *Ibid.*, 652, 655.

continued through later sessions. Gallatin shone in the debate. He presented the case of the United States with a clarity and a cogency that had never been given it before and that continued to illumine it in all the later Oregon negotiations. He showed that the United States had claims to the whole valley of the Columbia, the adjacent seaboard, and much more. But he concentrated his argument on the country between the 42nd and 49th parallels. His case was based on a variety of grounds, of which discovery was one. Discovery of the mouth of a river was recognized in the civilized world as giving the nation of the discoverer claims of sovereignty to the entire valley of the river and to the adjacent seaboard. Gallatin demonstrated that Britain had relied in the past on this principle. He showed, from the testimony of Vancouver, that Gray had discovered the mouth of the Columbia. He also proved that the interior waters of the river had been first explored by Americans—by the Lewis and Clark expedition. With regard to the waters washing the southern end of Vancouver Island he showed that their discovery had been a gradual process in which traders and explorers of various nations, Spanish, British, and American, had shared. Vancouver had encountered Spanish explorers in the Gulf of Georgia at the time of his great survey, and they had accompanied him around the island. The United States had acquired all the rights created by Spanish exploration.

To the rights derived from discovery the United States had added, as Gallatin showed, those of colonization. Americans had established Astoria at the mouth of the Columbia and other posts in the interior. Though Astoria had been taken by British arms in the War of 1812, it had been later restored to the United States in accordance with the Treaty of Ghent. The United States also had rights, Gallatin maintained, that derived from the contiguity of its territory to that which was in dispute. Between parallels of latitude 42° and 49° the United States adjoined the Pacific Northwest. It was the land mass of which the Pacific Northwest was the extension. From the United States would come, in the not distant future, the population which would occupy that wilderness. Gallatin showed that the civilized world, and England especially, gave adherence to the principle that contiguity creates territorial rights. He demonstrated that the British sea-to-sea charters of the colonial period in America had been based on this principle. His argument throughout was a masterly combination of cogency of reasoning and moderation of statement.[3]

The British case was addressed to the thesis that no nation had a sound claim to sovereignty in the Oregon Country, that the region was still a no-man's land, open to all comers, and that it would go, and should go, to the power that occupied it. The British made a point of not even claiming rights of exclusive sovereignty there. They claimed merely limited rights, which they defended on grounds of prior discovery and occupation. They had taken this position as against Spain in the Nootka Sound controversy of 1790. They had departed from it momentarily in their negotiation with Gallatin in 1818 when they had claimed rights of exclusive sovereignty.[4] Now they were returning to their earlier position, a position easier to defend. They had no very good claim south of the straits, certainly not as strong a claim as that which the United States held after acquiring the rights of Spain. Their emphasis on rights of occupation accorded well with the fur-trade position they had been developing in Oregon after the War of 1812.

The arguments used in support of this British thesis were partly those of prior discovery. The achievements of British explorers south of 49° on the coast were emphasized, especially those of Drake, Cook, Meares, and Broughton. Meares was shown to have been at the mouth of the Columbia before Gray, though it had to be conceded he had failed to recognize the nature of the opening he had seen. Broughton was shown to have sailed farther up the Columbia than Gray. The explorers whose discoveries in the waters about Vancouver Island were

[3] *Ibid.,* 652-655, 666-671; also Huskisson and Addington to Canning, Nov. 23, 1826, F.O. 5: 219.

[4] Gallatin to Clay, August 7, 1827, *ASP, FR,* VI, 693.

stressed were Barkley, Dixon, and Vancouver. The explorations and settlements which had been made in the interior by the North West Company were also cited. The discovery Gray had made of the mouth of the Columbia was challenged on the ground not only that he had been preceded by Meares, but that he had been a mere private adventurer. The Spanish claims held by the United States were challenged on three grounds: that exploration had not been followed in the case of Spain by permanent settlements; that Spain, by the Nootka Sound convention, had abandoned her claim to exclusive sovereignty on the Northwest Coast;[5] and that her claims must in any event be regarded as conflicting with and weakening the United States claims, rather than as supplementing them. The British case was set forth in a formal statement, incorporated later in the protocols. It was probably drawn with a view to publication at an early date in the documentary series of Congress.

The British effected a quiet retreat in the course of this argument. They all but formally acknowledged the sovereignty of the United States in the region south of the Columbia. They not only presented no defence of their claim on that side; they called the attention of Gallatin to the fact that the Astoria site had been abandoned by the Hudson's Bay Company and that a new fort had been erected by the Company on the north side.[6] They were acting in this on the principle Canning had enunciated to Liverpool in his letter of the preceding July, that England would strengthen her claim north of the Columbia by exhibiting a willingness to yield ground on the southern side.

In the argument of both sides the principle of convenience was invoked. It was invoked chiefly against the proposals the opposite side made. The British brought it to bear against the American proposal of the 49th parallel to the sea. They showed that that line would sever the tip of Vancouver Island

[5] *ASP, FR*, VI, 662-666.
[6] *Ibid.*, 651.

and place the entire straits south of the truncated island within the United States. Gallatin invoked the same principle against the British proposal of the Columbia River line. He showed that the channel of the lower Columbia for a considerable distance runs close to the north shore, so close, that if the river were made the boundary the British would have complete control of its navigation. He pointed out also that on the whole Northwest Coast, from the northern boundary of California to Juan de Fuca Strait, not a single port deep enough for an American naval station was to be found; that the port at the mouth of the Columbia was unusable, because of the bar, except for light vessels of commerce; that north of the 49th parallel the coast abounded in harbors suitable for naval stations; that if all the deep-water harbors inside the straits were to pass to England, the exclusive naval command of the Northwest Coast would pass to England with them.[7] This argument was a strange one to come from the lips of a man who a few months earlier had been urging Adams and Clay to yield to the British all the waters in the Gulf of Georgia and the strait of Juan de Fuca. The argument was Gallatin's discharge of an obligation imposed by his instructions. Privately, in all probability, he deemed it academic. He was one of those who believed that an independent republic would rise in the Pacific Northwest, which would take over the harbors there, south as well as north, of the 49th parallel.[8]

While this debate was going on the British Cabinet was considering behind the scenes Gallatin's combined offer of the 49th parallel and the Columbia River navigation. It decided to reject the offer. The decision represented Canning's unwillingness to yield the lower river to the United States. It reflected also British objection to the conditional nature of the river navigation proposal.[9]

[7] Gallatin to Clay, Nov. 25, 1826, *ibid.*, 654-655.

[8] Grant and Addington to Dudley, August 6, 1827, F.O. 5: 230. Two reports were made to Dudley on this day; the one here cited was private.

[9] Gallatin to Clay, Nov. 25, 1826, *ASP, FR*, VI, 652-655.

In announcing the rejection the British plenipotentiaries indicated that they intended to make a counteroffer. They inquired of Gallatin first, however, whether he was authorized to deviate from the 49th parallel as a boundary. This was an improper probing into his instructions, but Gallatin, sensing that it was intended to open the way for a new offer, chose not to rebuke it. He replied that he must adhere to the 49th parallel as a basis. But he would entertain a proposal for deviation from this basis, designed for mutual convenience, provided it was consistent with the basis. Any deviation made to the south must be compensated for by an equivalent at the north. Gallatin did not indicate the nature of the deviation he had in mind, but he later wrote Clay that he intended an exchange of the southern extremity of Vancouver Island for part or all of the valley of the Columbia north of 49°.[10]

The British followed this lead with their new proposal, which contained a concession beyond the traditional offer of the line of the Columbia. They proposed to concede to the United States, in the region adjoining Juan de Fuca Strait, a quadrilateral of territory, a detached tract, comprising roughly the Olympic Peninsula. The tract was to be bounded on the north by the strait of Juan de Fuca; on the west by the ocean; on the south by a line drawn from a point south of Gray's Harbor to Hood's Canal; on the east by Hood's Canal and Admiralty Inlet to the straits. The offer was intended to give the United States a portion of the deep-water harbors inside the straits, especially Port Discovery, which Vancouver had described as particularly excellent.[11]

The offer was doubtless a compromise in the Cabinet—a

[10] Gallatin to Clay, Dec. 2, 1826, *ibid.*, 655-656.

[11] Canning had instructed the British plenipotentiaries to offer Gallatin at the outset merely the harbor of Port Discovery, with a semicircle of territory around it five miles in radius. This instruction they carried out. Only after the offer had been rejected by Gallatin "with some vivacity" did they make the final quadrilateral offer authorized by Canning. Of the initial offer and its rejection no record was made in the protocol (Canning to Huskisson and Addington, Nov. 30, 1826, F.O. 5: 219; Huskisson and Addington to Canning, Dec. 7, 1826, F.O. 5: 219; *ASP, FR,* VI, 656, 660).

compromise between the views of Liverpool and those of Canning. It was an attempt to satisfy the American demand for a deep-water harbor inside the straits without loosening the British grip on the lower Columbia. As an added attraction, the British proposed that neither state should ever in the future erect works at the entrance to or on the banks of the Columbia which would impede the free navigation of the river.

As a bid for agreement the offer was woefully inadequate. It was the offer of an enclave. It was the presentation, for an American naval station, of an isolated tract of land hemmed in on every side by British territory or by water that would be dominated by the British navy. Gallatin at once rejected the offer. He declared that even to take it for reference to his government would be inconsistent with his instructions.[12]

As a rejected offer it now became a recording problem. It was made so by the British. They wished to exclude all record of it from the minutes of the conference. They wished the offer to be regarded as having been informally made. Gallatin would have agreed to this, but he was further asked to agree to a positive statement in the protocol that no new offer had been made. He resisted such a statement as contrary to the truth. The British finally relented and agreed that the offer should be recorded as made, though with a reservation that it was not to be regarded as prejudicing their position in the future.[13]

The offer did prejudice their position in the future. Its very presence on the protocol, notwithstanding the reservation to the contrary, formed a precedent of concession north of the Columbia. What was more significant, it revealed British irresolution in defending their position north of the river. Canning, having won his triumph over Liverpool three weeks before, had now abandoned it. He had warned the premier that the Cabinet must

[12] See the references cited in the footnote above.

[13] Gallatin to Clay, Dec. 5, 1826, *ASP, FR*, VI, 657; Gallatin to Addington, Dec. 4, 1826, Gallatin Papers, Bundle 9. The British plenipotentiaries wrote Canning that they permitted the offer to be recorded because they wished to display in the protocol the government's "earnest desire to accommodate matters" (Huskisson and Addington to Canning, Dec. 7, 1826, F.O. 5: 219).

maintain its position immovably at the Columbia. "If we retreat from that," he had predicted, "the cession of Astoria will have been but the first symptom of weakness, the first of a series of compliances with encroachments, which, if not resisted, will grow upon success." In agreeing to the enclave offer, Canning had himself retreated; he had himself betrayed a symptom of weakness; he had contributed to a "series of compliances with encroachments" which prepared the way for the later advance of the United States to the line of the 49th parallel.

In the meantime, after Gallatin's refusal even to refer the enclave offer to his government, the conference recognized that it could reach no agreement to partition the Oregon Country. It decided to stop trying. It turned, instead, to the more modest undertaking of continuing the convention of joint occupation of 1818. That convention, a ten-year covenant, was due to expire in two more years. To the task of renewing it the conference turned at its third session.

CHAPTER VII

THE NEGOTIATION: JOINT OCCUPATION

As soon as the conference turned to the task of renewing the convention of joint occupation a complication appeared. The complication was a British proposal to insert into the convention an interpretative stipulation in the form of a second article and to make the acceptance of it by the American government a condition of the renewal. The stipulation was that neither contracting party, during the lifetime of the convention, would "assume or exercise any right of exclusive sovereignty or dominion over any part of the said [Oregon] country, nor form therein any establishment in support or furtherance of any such claim."[1]

The meaning of the stipulation was spelled out for Gallatin by the British. The key word in it was the word "exclusive." If the stipulation were accepted, the right to assume or exercise any exclusive sovereignty or dominion over any part of the Oregon Country would be renounced by the two governments. The right to establish any military post in that country would be given up. Initially Gallatin understood that only a military post exclusively commanding the mouth of the Columbia River would be regarded by the British as an infraction of the stipulation, but later it became clear that any American military post which was government-established would be regarded as a violation of the agreement. The establishment of a distinct territorial government by either power over the Oregon Country would also be ruled out. Each government, however, would retain the right to extend its territorial laws over its own nationals in this wilderness, though not over the nationals of the other, and each would retain the right to try, and to punish, its own nationals for offenses committed there. Any impediment to the free navigation of harbors and rivers, any levying of duties or establishment of

[1] *ASP, FR*, VI, 657.

customs houses, any removing or disturbing of the settlements of either party by the other, would be infractions of the stipulation; though, as Gallatin, in a letter home observed, they would have been infractions under the existing convention without the stipulation. The net effect of the stipulation would have been, if approved, the renunciation by either party of the right to erect any military post or establish any distinct territorial government in the Oregon Country during the lifetime of the convention.[2]

The stipulation was Canning's project. It was probably what he had in mind when first he proposed to the American government that an Oregon negotiation be held. He could not confidently have expected any boundary settlement, opposed as he was to the concessions that a settlement with the United States would have entailed. The stipulation could be hoped for; it could be made a condition of the renewal of the convention. The stipulation would satisfy immediate British purposes. It would give the Hudson's Bay Company time to fasten its grip on the region north of the Columbia. It would be the answer given to the agitation in Congress to erect an American military post at the mouth of the Columbia and an American territorial government over the whole of the Oregon Country. It would tie the hands of American Floyds for the term of the renewed convention.

A plausible argument was offered by the British plenipotentiaries for this plan. The argument was that the stipulation merely clarified the intent of the convention. The intent of the convention, the British said, was to suspend the right of exercising sovereignty in the Oregon Country. This was evident from the fact that the convention was an agreement of joint occupation, an agreement that the Oregon Country should be free and open to the nationals of both parties. No nation, in any case, the British said, ever had rights of exclusive sovereignty in the Oregon Country. Such rights would some day come to the nation that settled the country.[3]

[2] Gallatin to Clay, Dec. 20, 1826, *ibid.*, 658-659.
[3] Gallatin to Clay, Dec. 5, 1826, August 7, 10, 1827, *ibid.*, 657, 691, 694.

With the question of the stipulation the British connected the question of the term for which the convention should be renewed. The term that Canning would have favored if the stipulation could have been agreed upon was fifteen or twenty or even twenty-five years instead of ten. The lengthened term would fit well into the purposes of the Hudson's Bay Company.

Gallatin met the stipulation proposal as his instructions required. He referred it to his government. He had been directed to refer to Washington any British proposal that involved a substantial change in the convention; he was authorized to agree only to a simple renewal for a ten year period.[4] He sent the proposal home in December 1826. He received the reply of the President, through Clay, in March of the following year. The reply was a rejection in unequivocal terms of the proposal. The delivery of the reply was delayed until the end of May, owing to the cabinet crisis in England caused by Liverpool's illness and retirement.[5]

Despite the rejection Canning still had hopes that the stipulation might be vendible. He offered it in a new dress. On June 19 Gallatin was informed by the British plenipotentiaries that a simple renewal of the convention for a period of ten years would be acceptable—but only on the condition that a declaration em-

---

[4] Gallatin did suggest, however, omitting from the convention the clause referring to "claims of any other Power or State," which had been written into the instrument originally as a protection to Spain and Russia. He believed that this clause had become obsolete as a result of the treaties the two powers had made. His suggestion was not approved by the British, who preferred to adhere to the thesis that the Oregon Country was a vacant region, open to all comers.

Gallatin also made the suggestion informally that only the "debateable ground" of the Oregon Country be put under the convention if it was revised, and that all the rest of that country be assigned at once in exclusive possession to one or the other of the two claimants. What he regarded as the "debateable ground" he did not say, but he wrote home that he had in mind the area north of 49°. The suggestion did not appeal to the British (Gallatin to Clay, Dec. 5, 12, 1826, *ASP, FR*, VI, 657, 658; Clay to Gallatin, Feb. 24, 1827, *ibid.*, 646-647; *ibid.*, 660; Huskisson and Addington to Canning, Dec. 7, 1826, F.O. 5: 219).

[5] *ASP, FR*, VI, 676; Adams, *Memoirs*, VII, 226.

bodying the British understanding of the convention be permitted to appear in the protocol: namely, that both parties were restricted "from exercising, or assuming to themselves the right to exercise, any exclusive sovereignty or jurisdiction over the territory mentioned in that article.[6]

Gallatin rejected this proposal. He pointed out that to admit this declaration into the protocol would be tantamount to inserting in the convention the stipulation which the American government had already given notice it could not accept. If the British were to insert this declaration into the protocol, it would become necessary for him to reply with a counterdeclaration, setting forth the American view of the convention. Of what avail would an agreement then be, accompanied by two declarations of such opposite character? He declared he would be unable to renew the convention if accompanied by any British declaration purporting to explain its meaning or intent.[7]

At this stage Gallatin was in a position to expound the American view of the meaning of the convention. He had been unable to do so while uncertain of the verdict of the President on the projected stipulation and had contented himself merely with expressing his preference for a simple renewal. He had the knowledge necessary for an authoritative exposition of the convention. He had been one of the authors of the instrument. He proceeded to analyze it with a clarity and force that on both sides of the Atlantic illumined the subject as long as the compact remained in effect.

The convention, he held, was what it appeared on its face to be, and nothing more. It was a commerce agreement, a free trade agreement, a compact of joint exploitation. Its intent was to keep the Oregon Country open to the commerce and settlement of the nationals of both parties, free from any obstruction by the government or subjects of either. On the issue of sov-

---

[6] *ASP, FR*, VI, 677, 678; Dudley to Huskisson and Addington, June 18, 1827, F.O. 5: 230.

[7] Gallatin to Clay, August 7, 1827. *ASP, FR*, VI, 691; Grant and Addington to Dudley, August 6, 1827, F.O. 5: 230.

ereignty the convention was silent. It left that issue where it had found it. By the convention neither party was precluded from exercising exclusive sovereignty in the Oregon Country so long as no interference occurred with the freedom of commerce and settlement of the other.[8] Gallatin was stating facts of history. He had been asked in the negotiation of 1818 by the British to agree to a declaration in the convention that neither party would exercise under it any sovereign or territorial authority in the Oregon Country against the other, and he had refused. He had taken the position that the convention was a commercial agreement. The convention had been kept deliberately silent on the issue of sovereignty.[9]

As for the erection of a military post in the Oregon Country, Gallatin held that it was forbidden to neither party by the convention. A military occupation would be an infraction only if it interfered with the freedom of commerce and settlement which the convention protected. The erection of a military post by the United States might become necessary for the safeguarding of American traders and settlers against Indians and lawless whites, or for the protection of the Indians themselves against aggression. Military posts, which Congress and the President had merely contemplated, the British already had in the stockaded forts and the powerful organization of the Hudson's Bay Company.[10]

A territorial government established by either party in the Oregon Country would, like a military post, be no infraction in itself of the convention. It would be an infraction only if it obstructed the freedom of trade and settlement which the convention assured. The United States might deem it necessary to

[8] Gallatin to Clay, August, 7, 1827, ASP, FR, VI, 691-693.

[9] See my article, "The Ghost River Caledonia in the Oregon Negotiation of 1818," AHR, LV (1949-50), 530-551. In 1821, when the first of the Floyd bills came before Congress, the British Cabinet decided that it did not conflict with the convention of joint occupation (Castlereagh to Stratford Canning, April 10, 1821, F.O. 116: 8; Canning to Stratford Canning, April 14, 1821, F.O. 116: 6). The Floyd bill is printed in Annals of Congress, 16 Cong., 2 sess. (1820-21), 958-59.

[10] Gallatin to Clay, August 7, 1827, ASP, FR, VI, 691-693.

form a territorial government in the Oregon Country as a means of maintaining order in a remote wilderness inhabited by savages and licentious traders. It would in that case be doing only what the British government had already done.

The British government had established the Hudson's Bay Company in the Oregon Country. To that company it had given a monopoly of British rights of trade. A powerful incorporated company, operating to the exclusion of private British traders, was in itself a territorial government. Through such agency Britain had long governed extensive and populous regions in the Orient. Experience in North America had shown that, where private British traders competed with each other for the peltry of savages, disorder and bloodshed occurred. When, however, there was an exclusive company, its agents governed; all other British subjects were its servants. All were kept in order and restrained from committing outrages on each other and on the Indians.[11]

Nothing was wanting then to a complete system of government but courts of law for the trial of criminal and civil cases. Such courts the British Parliament, in 1821, had established. A criminal and civil jurisdiction had been erected for certain parts of British North America and for the Oregon Country in the same act which authorized the monopoly given the Hudson's Bay Company. Courts for inferior criminal and civil cases, presided over by justices of the peace, had been established. Capital and other high offences, and all civil suits above a certain amount, had been placed under the jurisdiction of the courts of upper Canada. No provision had been made in the act for exempting citizens of the United States in the Oregon Country from this jurisdiction.[12]

The United States might have reason to complain of the act, Gallatin said, not as a breach of the convention of 1818, but as an infraction of the right of sovereignty claimed by the United States over the Oregon Country. If such complaint had not been made

[11] *Ibid.*
[12] *British Statutes,* 1 and 2 George IV, c. 66.

it was probably because the act had not been literally enforced.[13] But Great Britain, which had assumed as much jurisdiction as was necessary for protecting her subjects and maintaining order, could not complain if the United States adopted measures for the same object, even if the measures were not precisely the same as those Great Britain had found sufficient.

The American government could not create an incorporated monopoly in the Oregon Country. Incorporated monopolies were incompatible with the genius of American democratic institutions. The American mode of trade was competing companies and competing individuals. The American mode of control in a wilderness area was the territorial form of government. The United States might consider it necessary to establish a territorial form of government in the Oregon Country as a means of preserving peace and order among its citizens and giving them protection. Whatever the United States might contemplate in this respect, it had never yet actually exercised sovereignty or jurisdiction in that country. By this exposition Gallatin justified his government's rejection of the British proposal of a stipulation and his own rejection of the British project of a declaration in the protocol.[14]

The British were enough impressed with this exposition and the rejections to withhold further efforts to obtain a declaration on the issue of a territorial government. But they continued, as required by their instructions,[15] to press for a declaration on the issue of military posts. On June 26, at the eleventh conference, they announced that they would agree to a simple renewal of the convention, provided they could insert in the protocol one or the

[13] The act was apparently not known to the American government prior to 1827. Its adoption by Parliament seems to have escaped the notice of Rush. Its existence was discovered by Gallatin only in April, 1827. The British plenipotentiaries denied that the act was designed to apply to any except their own nationals in the Oregon Country. See Gallatin to Clay, April 21, 1827, State Department, England Despatches, xxxiii; same to same, August 7, 1827, *ASP, FR,* VI, 691-693; Huskisson and Addington to Dudley, June 8, 1827, F.O. 5: 230; Addington to Gallatin, June 20, 1827, Gallatin Papers, Private.

[14] Gallatin to Clay, June 22, 23, 1827, *ASP, FR,* VI, 677-678; 681-683.

[15] Dudley to Huskisson and Addington, June 18, 1827, F.O. 5: 230.

other of two declarations—(1) that the contracting parties had no right to take military possession of the Oregon Country, or (2) that if the United States did establish military posts in that country, Great Britain would do the same. They expressed a preference for the first of these declarations. The second might be construed in the United States as a threat. They declared that their government did not wish to erect military posts; it would do so only in self-defence.[16]

Gallatin at once rejected this proposal. He informed the British that he could not agree to a renewal of the convention if accompanied by any declaration in the protocol attaching any construction or interpretation whatever to the agreement. The proper place for such a declaration was not the protocol, but a communication addressed by the British government to the American government through the ordinary diplomatic channels.[17]

It was clear by now that the campaign of the British to write their own interpretation into the convention would not succeed. In the course of the debate one position after another had been taken by them only to be abandoned. The end had now clearly come. Renewal of the convention, *totidem verbis*, or no convention at all, had become the choice. The British protested to Gallatin that a convention of joint occupation, renewed without definition and known to mean opposite things to the signatories, would be hardly better than no convention at all. Inwardly they felt it would be somewhat better. A convention, amicably made and signed, even if without definition, would place a moral restraint on American aggression. The undefined convention had served British purposes well enough in the past. It had been a factor in preserving peace in the Oregon Country. It had permitted British fur companies to maintain their domination of that country. It would be likely to be of even greater utility in the future. A reorganized and reinvigorated Hudson's Bay Com-

---

[16] Gallatin to Clay, June 27, 1827, *ASP, FR,* VI, 680; Grant and Addington to Dudley, August 6, 1827, F.O. 5: 230.

[17] *Ibid.*

pany was at the beginning of a new program of expansion.

On July 21, after every hope of agreement on a declaration in the protocol had vanished, the British plenipotentiaries made their final move. They informed Gallatin that they would accept a simple renewal of the convention, though in view of the American rejection of the stipulation, they would agree to it only on a short-term basis. The short-term basis had become preferable since it would permit the convention to be quickly terminated on evidence that the United States had embarked on a plan of military occupation of the Oregon Country. The British also suggested that they would give consideration to any form of a temporary renewal Gallatin might wish to propose.[18]

Gallatin readily approved the principle of a short term renewal. He also suggested the form. The British had shortly before proposed that the commercial convention of 1815 be renewed for an indefinite period, subject to the condition that it could be terminated on a twelve-months' notice by either party. That form, Gallatin suggested, should be applied to the convention of joint occupation. This was acceptable to the British. On August 6 the convention, so framed, was engrossed and signed. Its renewal had been a labor of eight months.[19]

[18] *ASP, FR,* VI, 687; Grant and Addington to Dudley, August 6, 1827, F.O. 5: 230.

[19] Gallatin to Clay, August 7, 9, 1827, *ASP, FR,* VI, 691-694. The August 7 dispatch is an admirable brief résumé of the negotiation.

CHAPTER VIII

THE PEACEMAKER

In the course of the months of negotiation Gallatin had come increasingly to feel that something more than the renewal of the naked convention was needed to safeguard the peace in the Oregon Country. He considered the Canning stipulation no sufficient safeguard—it would merely restrict the rival exercise of exclusive sovereignty. What was needed was an agreement regulating in specific terms the relations between the two occupying powers in the Oregon Country—a field contract for the period of the joint occupation. In referring home the Canning stipulation Gallatin had suggested that he be given authority to conclude such an agreement. He had been disappointed when the President had authorized merely the renewal of the convention. He believed that an opportunity had been lost. He had loyally carried out the President's wishes, but he continued to feel that a supplementary agreement was necessary.

To pave the way for such an agreement Gallatin had carried on informal conversations with the British plenipotentiaries and with Canning while the formal negotiations were still in progress. These conversations are a significant phase of the conference. They throw light on the nature of the joint occupation and the problems which it raised. They exhibit Gallatin in his characteristic role of peacemaker and they make more understandable his proceedings in the conference. The recordings of the conversations are British and must be used with caution, since they are *ex parte,* colored perhaps by British prepossessions, and catch ideas in the process of evolution.[1]

---

[1] Two letters reporting these conversations were sent to the Foreign Office by the British plenipotentiaries, both of the same date. One is official, the other unofficial. The official report is Grant and Addington to Dudley, August 6, 1827, No. 6, F.O. 5: 230. The unofficial report (*ibid.*), the more valuable of the two, carries no dispatch number.

The recordings show that Gallatin, on June 9, some months after the arrival of the letter from home ordering a mere renewal of the convention, confided to the British that he believed citizens of the one nation, apprehended in the commission of crime within the limits or possessions of the other in the Oregon Country, should be transferred by their captors to the other to be dealt with under the laws and tribunals of their own government. On the same occasion he evidently also expressed the opinion that it might be inexpedient for the United States to erect military posts in the Oregon Country. He added, to quote the British report,

that it would surely be the greatest folly imaginable for two powers like Great Britain and the United States to be quarrelling about a matter of such very minute present interest to either. In the United States it would be still greater absurdity than in Great Britain, since in the natural course of things, if Great Britain were not forced into colonizing the country, it must necessarily, from its proximity to the United States, fall eventually into the hands of that Power, or rather, Mr. Gallatin said, it would fall into the hands of neither. It would be peopled by both, but mainly by the United States, and would eventually, as its population and internal organization advanced, render itself independent of both.[2]

At a later conference he returned to the subject of the military posts. He was reported to have said that he did not see how the United States could dispense entirely with such a post in the Oregon Country. One would be needed to give support and protection to American citizens who would settle in that country. He thought an agreement might be reached permitting each nation to establish one such post, the size of its garrison to be limited.

Gallatin was reported to have felt that an interval of time was

[2] The conviction that an independent republic would arise in the Pacific Northwest remained with Gallatin throughout the life of the joint occupation agreement. It was asserted by him in 1846, at the height of the Oregon crisis, in the concluding letter of a series originally published in the *National Intelligencer,* and subsequently republished as a pamphlet. See Albert Gallatin, *Letters on the Oregon Question* (Washington, 1846), No. 5. Alexander Baring also adhered to the same view to the end.

necessary before a new agreement should be attempted. Issues had been raised by the proposed British stipulation that required further study. On both sides of the Atlantic the national temper was unfavorable at the moment to a calm and dispassionate consideration of the problem. In the United States, Congress and the people, with scarcely an exception, regarded the American claim to the Oregon region as indefeasible, as admitting neither doubt nor dispute, and the British claim as a deliberate and unjust aggression on it. But when the clouds which at present enveloped the issue had had time to clear away, he did not despair of some more substantial and definite arrangement being concluded.[3]

Gallatin sought to prepare his own government in the same way for a new negotiation. He sent Clay, shortly after signing the convention, a long letter devoted to this problem, which was designed for the eyes of the President. The letter is one of the most revealing documents of the negotiation.[4] It opens with a statement, made "with confidence," that the British government had no wish at present to colonize the Oregon Country; that they viewed that country with indifference; that they believed when it was settled it would not long remain a colony either of Britain or of the United States; and that they were willing to let the settlement of it take its natural course.

However, they would not be prepared to agree now, nor for some time in the future, to such a partition of it as the United States desired and had a right to claim. They would not be supported in doing so by British public opinion. The Hudson's Bay Company, though perhaps less favored now than it had once been, would continue to be the principal bar to a partition settlement. Such a partition as would be satisfactory to the United States would not be possible until the citizens of the United States had acquired a respectable footing in that country.

In the meantime the British government would feel itself bound to protect existing establishments created by British capital and enterprise. Recollections of the high ground assumed

[3] See the references in Chapter VI, note 8.
[4] Gallatin to Clay, August 10, 1827, *ASP, FR,* VI, 694-696.

by Britain toward Spain in the Nootka affair would have their influence, and national pride would prevent any abrupt relinquishment of British claims. But Great Britain "did not seem indisposed to let the country gradually and silently slide into the hands of the United States"; and she was anxious that it should not, in any event, become the cause of a rupture with the United States.

As evidence that the British government was willing to permit the disputed region silently to "slide" into American possession Gallatin cited the fact that the British plenipotentiaries had sedulously avoided in the negotiation setting up a claim to exclusive sovereignty over any part of the Oregon Country; that they had reverted, instead, to the doctrine advanced in the Nootka affair of a wilderness unoccupied and open to all. Such an exposition of the nature of the British claim, Gallatin thought, was far more significant than any of the arguments advanced by the British in support of it.[5]

Since Great Britain would permit the region to pass to the United States, provided peace were preserved, it was important for the American government to consider the measures necessary to prevent conflicts. A number of these were suggested in Gallatin's letter for the President's consideration. The desires expressed in Congress for an American territorial jurisdiction in the Oregon Country, Gallatin felt, could be satisfied without any formal agreement. On this issue, he observed, the British had at first been particularly sensitive. He had relieved their apprehensions in great part by the explanations he had given and the comparisons he had made of the British and American modes of extending jurisdiction. He thought the issue could be arranged by extending the jurisdiction of an established territory of the United States over the trans-mountain country and defining the country over which the jurisdiction was extended in general terms similar to those used in the act of Parliament of 1821.

On three issues, Gallatin felt, a definite agreement should be made. From his informal talks with the British he could report

[5] *Ibid.* Also same to same, Dec. 20, 1826, ibid., 658.

what the British desires on these issues were. The first was an agreement that no customs house should be erected nor any duties raised by either party on tonnage, merchandise, or commerce in the region west of the Rockies.[6] This restriction, he thought, was already implied in the convention—in the requirement that the country be free and open to the vessels, citizens, and subjects of the two powers. He observed that the extension of the revenue laws of the United States to that quarter would be undesirable, that if duties were exacted on merchandise intended for the Indian trade, the citizens of the United States would not be able to compete with the Hudson's Bay Company.

The second measure proposed was that the citizens and subjects of the two powers in the Oregon Country should be amenable only to the jurisdiction of the courts of their own nation. Gallatin believed that an agreement on this subject was indispensable. Without one, it would hardly be possible to avoid collisions.

The third measure desired by the British was an agreement that no military post be established by either power in the Oregon Country. Gallatin thought that this was the most difficult part of the whole problem. He wrote that he had repeatedly explained to the British, with some effect he had at first believed, why Great Britain could dispense with a military force in the Oregon Country while the United States could not. In the later discussions, however, it was the point on which they had been most tenacious. The establishment of a military post, they felt, would be a formal national occupation, and one of such notoriety that Great Britain could not permit it to be done without following suit. If the United States built forts, Great Britain indubitably would do the same. The real objection, from the American point of view, to embarking on a race of armaments would then

[6] The Floyd bills of 1821 and 1824 each included an authorization to the President to open a port of entry within the Oregon Country and to extend the revenue laws of the United States to it. The bill of 1824 extended the revenue laws to the whole area west of the Rocky Mountains and north of 42° without specifying a northern boundary. See Chapter I, note 12, and Chapter VII, note 9.

appear. Great Britain, with a far greater military establishment than the United States, could, without much inconvenience, send out larger detachments for service to Oregon. And if Great Britain did once take military possession, the result, quite apart from the danger of collisions, would be that she would find it much more difficult to withdraw voluntarily at a later time from the area she had occupied.[7]

The thesis in Gallatin's letter that the British viewed the Oregon region with indifference and were willing to permit it to slide into American possession in the future was doubtless based on conversations with members of the British government. It is entitled to the respect due the judgment of a highly competent observer, and it did represent views in some circles in British politics. But it could not have represented the views of Canning, and if Canning persuaded Gallatin to the contrary, he was another of the diplomats of that generation who practiced the arts of the real-estate agent.

The action taken by the British and American governments on Gallatin's plan was to shelve it. The plan had been designed for the future; it was relegated to the indefinite future. In England, Canning died two days after the signing of the convention; the government that succeeded him was an interim one without energy. In the United States, Adams was in no mood to make concessions on the Oregon issue to the British. Even if he had been, his administration was moving toward a close. He was beset in Congress by a factional opposition of extraordinary virulence, which would have flayed him if he had agreed to Gallatin's suggestions.

Throughout the negotiation Gallatin had been trying to lead the two governments on the road to a real peace. He had been the reconciler, the seeker of compromise. He had been manifesting his conviction that the diplomatist is more than the advocate of national gain, that he is also the minister of peace. He had been almost internationalist in outlook, Swiss rather than Yankee. He had sought initially to narrow the gap between national

[7] The above account is a paraphrasing of the report of Gallatin.

demands and to bridge it. When this proved impossible, he had sought to build a basis for a secure truce. His labors were the expression of an innate cosmopolitanism and a spirit of moderation. They were the result of his eagerness for Anglo-American reconciliation. They were perhaps also a response to his conviction, shared with his lifelong friend Alexander Baring, that the region west of the Rockies would become an independent republic. But even Gallatin could not reconcile the conflicting desires of a Canning and an Adams, each representing an extreme and irascible nationalism.

CHAPTER IX

CONCLUSION

The conference closed in September 1827. It closed with an output hardly commensurate with the year and a half of planning and discussion that had gone into its sessions. The sum of its achievement was the renewal of two conventions—joint occupation and the commercial convention of 1815—and an agreement to refer the issue of the northeast boundary to the decision of some friendly sovereign. The prime object of the negotiation, at least ostensibly—the partition of the Oregon Country—had failed.

Yet the negotiation, even in its Oregon phase, was not a complete failure. It was a success in that it lowered tensions which had developed to the danger point on the opposite sides of the ocean. In the United States the feeling had become virtually unanimous that the British case in the Oregon Country was meritless, that their presence south of 49° was a sheer encroachment, that containment of them was a vital need. In Congress the limitationists, who wished to reserve the Oregon area for a new republic, and the expansionists, who desired to acquire it for the United States, had joined forces and were moving irresponsibly toward a showdown with the British. Misinterpreting the quietness of the British press and Parliament,[1] and encouraged by the 1824 message of President Monroe, they had put through the House by an overwhelming majority the Floyd bill which was designed to push the British from the Oregon Country. In England, Canning was storing up wrath. He regarded the noncolonization doctrine of the American executive and the militant proceedings of Congress as all of one piece—to expel Britain from a country where he had

---

[1] Addington to Canning, May 2, 1826, F.O. 5: 221.

ambitions for the British Empire.[2] In 1826 he was, if not yet in a mood for a rupture with the United States, at least in what Adams described as a "waspish" mood.[3] That mood was reflected at the conference in the excessive "susceptibility" which Gallatin described the British plenipotentiaries as exhibiting in the Oregon discussions, and in the repeated warnings that they issued to Gallatin of the seriousness with which any aggressive action taken by Congress would be regarded by the British government.[4]

This explosiveness was reduced by the negotiation. It was reduced partly by the conciliatory temper and moderation brought by Gallatin to the discussions. It was reduced further by the forceful yet tactful presentation he made of the American claim to the Oregon Country and the American conception of the intent of the joint agreement. Canning and Huskisson and the Cabinet were undoubtedly given an education on this issue in the course of the negotiation.

A similar education was effected in the United States. The Adams administration and its successors were taught by the reports of Gallatin the unwisdom, from an American point of view, of any congressional measure that would drive England into a military occupation of the Oregon Country. The public in the United States was similarly educated. The education was hastened by a tradition of American democracy that the documents of important negotiations with foreign states should be promptly published. In 1828 the documents of the Oregon negotiation were submitted by Adams to Congress and were published.[5] In the protocols appeared the elaborate defense by the British of their claim, prepared in all probability with a view to its publication in the United States. The protocols made clear the sobering fact that Britain would fight if aggressive action were taken by Congress on the Oregon issue.

[2] Gallatin to Clay, Dec. 20, 1826, *ASP, FR,* VI, 658-659.

[3] Adams to Gallatin, Dec. 12, 1827, Gallatin, *Writings,* II, 398.

[4] Gallatin to Clay, Nov. 25, 1826, *ASP, FR,* VI, 652-654; same to same, Nov. 27, 1826, State Department, England, Despatches, xxxiii.

[5] 20 Cong., I sess. (1827-28), *H. Documents,* No. 199.

It was probably no accident that congressional agitation on the issue tapered off after the negotiation.[6] It was certainly no accident that the agitation was no longer fed by messages from American presidents. By 1830 a quiescent stage in the controversy had been reached, which continued to the end of the decade. It was not until the 1840's, until the movement of American pioneers into the Oregon Country had attained considerable proportions, with resulting political agitations, that the Oregon issue again became explosive.

In the meantime the convention of joint occupation justified the faith which Canning had placed in it. It permitted the Hudson's Bay Company to dominate the whole Oregon Country, south as well as north of the Columbia River. The Oregon Country became a British sphere of influence and remained so, uncontested to the end of the fur-trade era.

Such a result Adams undoubtedly foresaw when he agreed to the renewal of the convention. The Senate similarly foresaw it in ratifying the agreement. American fur traders operating on a small scale in the Oregon Country could not hope by their individual competition to displace a great British corporation. They had not done so in the case of the North West Company which had held the Oregon region to 1821. Still less could they hope to do so against a mammoth corporation such as the Hudson's Bay Company.

The American government, nevertheless, was acting with hard-headed and far-sighted realism in renewing the convention. Adams and the Senate recognized that whether or not the convention was renewed the Hudson's Bay Company would remain a fixture in the Oregon Country. Military action alone could loosen such a grip with any promptness, and military action the

[6] In the session of 1828-29, when the last of the Floyd bills was brought before the House, the attack on it was led by persons who relied for their ammunition on the published documents of the 1826-27 negotiation. The ablest speech by far against the bill was made by James K. Polk, the future president. It was an exposition almost entirely of the conflicts between the bill and the renewed convention in terms of information taken from the published documents of the negotiation. The bill was decisively defeated by the House. See *Congressional Debates*, 20 Cong., 2 sess. (1828-29), 129-132.

United States was not prepared to resort to. If the convention were permitted by the American government to lapse, the Hudson's Bay Company would remain in the Oregon Country despite the claims and rights of the United States. If the convention were renewed, the Company would be there by American sufferance.

From the point of view of the American government the renewal of the convention was a wise adjournment of a controversy. It was an adjournment to the day when the Oregon Country would be occupied by American settlers. To Gallatin this was what the renewal meant. It was what he had in mind in reporting to his government that no satisfactory boundary line would be obtainable "until the citizens of the United States shall have acquired a respectable footing in the country."[7] It was what Adams had in mind, also. On March 20, 1827, in a letter to Gallatin in which the failure of the partition negotiation was discussed, he referred at some length to the intransigeance of the British and the uncompromising spirit of Congress and concluded: "In this temper of the parties, all we can hope to accomplish will be to adjourn controversies which we cannot adjust, and say to Britain, as the Abbé Bernis said to Cardinal Fleuri, 'Monseigneur, j'attendrai.' "[8]

[7] Gallatin to Clay, August 10, 1827, *ASP, FR*, VI, 694. Gallatin made the following prediction regarding the advance of American settlement into the Oregon Country in his statement of the claims of the United States, delivered to the British, December 19, 1826: "Under whatever nominal sovereignty that country may be placed, and whatever its ultimate destinies may be, it is nearly reduced to a certainty that it will be almost exclusively peopled by the surplus population of the United States. The distance from Great Britain, and the expense incident to emigration, forbid the expectation of any being practicable from that quarter but on a comparatively small scale. Allowing the rate of increase to be the same in the United States and in the North American British possessions, the difference in the actual population of both is such that the progressive rate which would within forty years, add three millions to these, would, within the same time, give a positive increase of more than twenty millions to the United States. And if circumstances, arising from localities and habits, have given superior facilities to British subjects of extending their commerce with the natives, and to that expansion which has the appearance, and the appearance only, of occupancy; the slower but sure progress and extension of an agricultural population will be regulated by distance, by natural obstacles, and by its own amount" (*ASP, FR*, VI, 670).

[8] Gallatin, *Writings*, II, 368.

INDEX